HOW TO BE
PRETTY
THOUGH
PLAIN

HOW TO BE
PRETTY
THOUGH
PLAIN

Mrs Humphry

The British Library

First published in 1899 by J. Bowden

This edition published in 2014 by
The British Library
96 Euston Road
London NW1 2DB

British Library Cataloguing in Publication Data
A catalogue record for this publication
is available from the British Library

ISBN 978 0 7123 5717 3

Printed in Hong Kong by
Great Wall Printing Co. Ltd

CONTENTS

HOW TO BE PRETTY
THOUGH PLAIN.

———◆◇◆———

INTRODUCTORY.

GIRLS that are merry and wise know
perfectly well that to be pretty is the
natural desire of the girlish
A natural desire. heart ; and they also know
that over-anxiety in the
matter, like making haste to be rich,
is likely to defeat its own end.

But there are ways of making the
best of oneself that are perfectly
natural and easy and harm-
Lawful devices. less, as opposed to the
elaboration of cosmetics
and hair dyes, artifices to which no
girls that are honest and true would
have recourse. Health has far more
influence on good looks
Health as a beautifier. than is generally realised.
Perfect health is inextri-
cably associated with the highest
physical development. Health, too,
influences the temper, and the temper
has much to do with fashioning the
features, not only in childhood and
girlhood, but all through life. Good

temper will not make a turned-up nose turn down, but it works wonders with the brow, the eyes, the corners of the lips. Without good health it is very difficult indeed to be amiable and good-tempered, and many a face is spoiled by a peevish, discontented expression that would be delightfully gay and bright if only health were good.

Temper and prettiness.

There is more in the science of good looks than meets the eye at first, and since I began to write this book I have begun to perceive that surface beauty has a close connection with the depths of mind and spirit. Not only the face but the figure indicates much of what goes on within, in that solitude which is the lot of every human being: "On our features the fine chisels of thought and emotion are continually at work," said Alexander Smith, an almost forgotten but delightful essayist. And do not our dispositions write themselves on our figures? The lazy slouch and lounge. The active carry themselves upright, alert and ready. The good-tempered smile and cushion themselves with comfortable outlines. The anxious and the bilious grow thin.

Unseen factors.

Disposition and the figure.

"With a great deal of sheet-lightning in her ways" said Carlyle of Mrs. Buller. Sheet-lightning, if carried too far in this style, is apt to induce an unbecoming condition of scragginess; but too much calm and quietude, *laisser-aller* and "let things be," tend to the acquisition of rust. So many good souls, in such comfortable bodies, are complacently rusting away! The pity of it!

Sheet-lightning and rust.

Every one of these attitudes of mind writes itself plainly on the exterior, and those who run may read. Even a child and a dog can read the countenance, and in many a sweet old face is inscribed, all unconsciously to the owner, the record of—

The mind a graving tool.

" That best portion of a good man's life,
  His little nameless, unremembered acts
  Of kindness and of love."

And in many a figure can be distinctly read pride or humility, boldness or modesty, self-reliance or abject weakness, without the aid of even a glimpse of the countenance.

In a measure we make our own faces and mould our own figures. The sources of beauty in either lie deep within us, and though we cannot wile away a single freckle, any more than we can add a cubit to our stature, we can be our own artificers in many ways.

We are our own architects.

9

INTRODUCTORY.

It is in the hope of pointing out some of the plainest and most direct routes through health and kindliness to good looks that this little book is written. And it is intended especially for the plain girl who feels her inferiority to her pretty friends, and is dejected and even humiliated, in her inmost thoughts, by her lack of beauty.

The aim of this book.

The plain girl.

She must not give herself up as hopeless, as many a plain girl does, scrape her hair back into an unsymmetrical bundle, have her clothes " cut out with a hatchet and put on with a pitchfork," ill-use her skin with coarse soaps and neglect her figure. Only a beauty may dare to do all this, and even the loveliest cannot afford it. The plainer the features, the more is care necessary, and I hope to show in succeeding pages that there are dozens of ways, every one of them consistent with health of body and a perfectly wholesome frame of mind, in which it is possible to obtain the laudable ambition, innate in every girlish or womanly heart, to be as pretty as possible.

Things she must not do.

It would be hard indeed if only the beautiful among girls and women should win admiration and affection. But it is by no means the case. A pleasant expression, a bright countenance, a graceful figure, a charming manner, and attention to details of dress and

Beauty not everything.

toilette may transform an originally plain girl into one who attracts wherever she goes. " What men can see in her, I cannot think," murmurs the neglected beauty, finding herself unaccountably deserted. It is not always that beauty is associated with charm of manner and a winning voice. When it is, the union is a strong one indeed. But there are better things than beauty, and if these are honestly pursued the plainest face will shine with a radiance from within. Too often this **Want of care.** brightness of look is obscured by want of care in externals. Why should a sweet smile suffer from a display of neglected teeth ? Or a lovely look be spoiled by a blotched and coarsened skin ? Yet these trifles tell, even against the highest beauty, that of expression.

It is the most lasting, and eminently cultivable. Cheerfulness and brightness, combined with the sympathetic softness that refrains from **Expression, the highest beauty.** displaying either aggressively at the wrong moment, are good. To encourage oneself in the enjoyment of simple pleasures is excellent. To live one's life to the full, realising its joys and not shirking its duties, is an essential part of the treatment. Nothing makes one feel or look more disagreeable or discontented than a consciousness of having failed in, or postponed, some duty that lay to hand. To neglect opportunities of amusement is foolish, so long as there is nothing reprehensible in the form they take. Idle, aimless lives are certain to impair very seriously the charm of the countenance. Work and sympathy are the two great essentials in the making of a beautiful countenance. Work and love, really, but the word "love" has been so hackneyed, so fretted with silly jests, so misapplied, so utterly misused, that one fears to write it in its true sense, viz.: the innate prompting to our duty to our neighbour, the loving-kindness that intuitively does unto others what we would they should do unto us.

The two essentials.

As to work, it is the sweetener of daily life to both men and women. It is the salt that saves existence from insipidity. It is the running tide without which the river of years would be but stagnant water. Mrs. Barrett Browning knew its supporting strength when she wrote—

In praise of work.

> " Get work ! get work !
> Be sure 'tis better than what you work to get."

Work well done has made many a plain face beautiful ; a small result were it not that this beauty is but a reflection from the spirit within, ennobled and redeemed from the pettiness of self by the self-denial, conscientious care, and integrity of spirit inseparable from the blessing into which humanity's primal curse has mercifully developed. Good work, honestly done, is a great beautifier. It not only ennobles the expression but refines the features if it is congenial work and not too arduous.

There is every excuse for a girl to wish to be pretty. If she opens a book of poems or a novel, she finds beauty bepraised and ugliness condemned. If she looks in at a picture gallery, or gazes at the photographs in a shop window, she finds the handsomest faces selected to be hung on the line. At the opera or theatre she sees the attention excited by a lovely face. In the Park she watches with appreciation the pretty faces and observes that others do so as well. Wherever she goes, in fact, the great truth, that pretty women are among the most sought after things on earth, is made patent to her.

The worship of beauty.

Small wonder, then, that the grand question in the young girl's mind is "Am I pretty?" And this often followed up with : "And if not, how best shall I circumvent my plainness?"

"Am I pretty?" a natural question.

Anxious as women usually are to be pretty and attractive, there are means of being so which are very often neglected. False and disengenuous methods are pursued, entailing endless difficulties, such as squeezing-in the waist,

Injurious methods.

13

darkening the eyebrows and lashes, dyeing the hair, plastering the skin with unguents and cosmetics, wearing false hair, and padding the figure ; but not one of them ever achieves a true success. Girls and women who use such means as these would often be surprised to hear that they neglect the greatest beautifier of all—true cleanliness. They stop up the **The value of cleanliness.** pores of the skin with rouge and powder, brush in sticky dyes into their hair, and, with evening dress, rub powder into their skin on the arms and shoulders. They thus defeat Nature's intention in the construction of the wonderful human skin, with its marvellous functions of bringing to the surface all that is injurious, ready to be thrown off, and its receptivity of air, light, and other factors in the healthful condition of the body.

THE COMPLEXION.

" There is a garden in her face
    Where roses and white lilies grow ;
A heavenly paradise is that place,
    Wherein all pleasant fruits do grow ;
There cherries grow that none may buy
Till cherry-ripe themselves do cry."
                            RICHARD ALISON.

        "Alas ! Now I see
The reason why fond women love to buy
Adulterate complexion ; here 'tis read
False colours last after the true be dead."
                            THOMAS DEKKER.

PART I.

FRESH AIR THE BEST COSMETIC.

WITHOUT fresh air the body cannot be
healthy, and in the absence of good
health the possibilities of
Value of fresh air. good looks are diminished.
Many a girl whose com-
plexion might be clear and softly tinted,
if she only gave it a chance, goes
through life with a thick and muddy-
looking skin, a hilly complexion that
suggests the advisability of an application of emery paper. And why ?
Because she insists on sleep-
Sleeping with closed windows. ing with windows shut, and
therefore breathes bad air
for at least three-quarters
of the night.

THE COMPLEXION.

Listen to what the scientists say. A room that measures 10 feet wide by 15 long and 20 high contains enough air Opinion of scientists. for the consumption of one person for one hour. After that its freshness is gone, owing to the carbonic acid given off by the lungs.

Now, if the freshness is gone at the end of one hour, in what condition will the air of the room be at the end From bad to worse. of two hours? three hours? four hours? And in the morning? It is terrible to think of. Yet the majority of persons sleep with their bedroom windows and doors shut. If only people would realise how fatally they sacrifice their health in this way, every bedroom window would be open every night and all night long.

But it is not only at night that windows are kept shut, even in summer. We Suburban stuffiness. once had occasion to drive round a suburb of London and through a number of streets on which the backs of some flats and a number of large houses looked out. We were astonished to notice how few of the windows were open. In most of the houses every one was fastened tightly up. There were probably windows open in the front of the houses, but in hot weather there should be as much fresh air as possible admitted — nay, invited — into every room.

The ideal room to live in is one which has a window at either end, so that a thorough draught of air can play through it in the absence of the occupants. I say, in their absence, for though fresh air, and plenty of it, is one of the first aids to health and beauty, draughts are highly dangerous.

The ideal room.

Even in winter, whenever possible, the windows of sitting-rooms should be thrown open. Directly the maids come down in the morning they should open the windows. Immediately upon the family leaving the dining-room after meals the windows should be thrown open. When they leave the drawing-room to proceed to the dining-room for lunch or dinner, then the drawing-room windows should be opened. In the same way, when the ladies of a family go out for a walk, or shopping, or making calls, they should see that the windows of the living-rooms are opened before they leave the house.

How to keep the house fresh.

The usual custom of having the gas lighted in bedrooms early in the evening and burning there till bedtime, convenient as it certainly is, is most injurious to health, and consequently to good looks. The gas vitiates the air, robbing it of its freshness and of those qualities which render it one of the principal nutrients of the body. It is

Burning gas in bedrooms.

infinitely better to banish gas from bed-rooms, or, failing that, to use it as little as possible. Even on the staircase, with three or four gas burners alight, the air becomes vitiated and stale. Lamps are much better, in default of the electric light.

A window should be kept open on the staircase in all but the coldest weather, to admit the fresh air and allow the stale to pass out.

Staircase windows.

We should so accustom ourselves to perfect purity in the air we breathe that a sense of discomfort becomes inseparable from being in a room where the air is almost exhausted of its oxygen. We can easily educate ourselves in this matter by doing our best to live constantly, night and day, in pure air.

Cultivating a fresh-air instinct.

Some people are very sensitive to impure air, and it is to be wished that all were so, not only for their own sake but for that of others. I have some-times been out in a brougham or cab with both windows tightly closed, in company with one or more persons who seemed to feel no disagreeable effects from the close atmosphere. And it might have been remedied in a moment, for by a merciful provision of Nature's laws the foul air rushes out and the fresh air rushes in immediately that a window is opened.

Nature's remedy.

A thorough draught is necessary for the perfect changing of the air in a large room. Both door and window should be set wide, the former being propped against the risk of banging. Door-banging is never permitted in a well-managed house.

A thorough draught.

The best mode of keeping a room constantly ventilated without draught is to have the frame of the lower part supplemented by an additional piece of wood, similar to the rest, about five inches deep. This admits of the lower sash being raised without any draught from the bottom of the window. Air is admitted in the middle, where the lower sash is raised above the end of the top one. This very seldom causes a draught, unless a cold wind should happen to be blowing that way, when the window should at once be shut down.

Ways and means.

It must not be imagined for a moment that the quality of the complexion depends only on the amount of pure air absorbed by the pores of the skin on the face only. On the contrary, every pore on the whole body contributes to the result. We breathe through the skin all over our bodies. If we take in bad air or insufficient air in this way, it soon tells on the face. If good, and plenty of it, it tells in a very different way. Man was not originally intended for a clothes-

Air for the body.

wearing animal. Nature meant him to take air in freely through all the pores of his skin. Our necessary **"Clothes and the man."** clothing robs us of much of this. But we can all dress lightly and suitably, instead of thickly and unsuitably, to these conditions. Most of us, and especially elderly people, wear far too much clothing. This is doubly harassing to **The misuse of garments.** the functions of the skin. Not only do the layers of garments prevent the air from getting to the pores and feeding them with what they need, but they also prevent the skin from throwing off and getting rid of those noxious exhalations which come to the surface and injure health if they cannot escape.

Too many clothes by day, and too many bedclothes at night, are the rule. We should accustom ourselves to the minimum of both, and never carry an unnecessary ounce. The bicycle has done good service in ridding **A good word for the bicycle.** women of superfluous underskirts. Before its time three were the rule, being one too many in winter and three too many in summer.

In hot weather one thin blanket should be quite sufficient, but this will not be found enough by those who have accustomed themselves **Too many blankets.** to sleep under four or five in winter. Thick clothing and supererogatory blankets prevent the skin from absorbing air, and also obstruct the cells, clogging them with their own secretions.

An air bath comes only second to a water bath in efficacy for the skin. **Air baths.** The face and hands are the only portions of the body that enjoy it daily. When possible, the whole surface of the skin should be exposed for a few moments to the action of the air in a room where the atmosphere is fresh. The few moments after a bath when the skin has been freed from soap and is glowing from the rubbing of the towel are valuable indeed, but this is little recognised. The refreshing influence of an air bath may be tested for itself, and after one or two trials it will be found so valuable that it will be enjoyed as often as possible. Those who suffer from insomnia should wash the body **Treatment for insomnia.** all over before going to bed, and leave the whole of the skin uncovered while they walk up and down the room after washing and drying. A nightgown not too thick—it is astonishing how some people can wear the thick ones they do!—and warm, light blankets will come into the conspiracy to defeat insomnia.

For the reason that air should have, so much as may be possible, free access to the skin, open-work **Hygienic foot-wear.** stockings are more hygienic than closely woven ones. Boots should be open work as well, but this would offer some considerable difficulty. Jaeger boots and shoes are ventilated, but none other that I know of.

The ideal clothing would be open-work, the number of layers being increased in order to afford **The ideal clothing.** full protection and covering to the skin.

This rather long lecture on ventilation may seem to have very little to do with being pretty ; but it is, **A means to an end.** in reality, a most important means to that end. Good ventilation will not, it is true, alter the shape of an unsatisfactory nose or turn thin lips into a Cupid's bow, but it will go far towards surrounding plain features with such attractive tinting of milk and roses as will render their defects scarcely observable.

THE COMPLEXION (Continued).

"All eyes may see from what the change arose,
All eyes may see—a pimple on her nose."

POPE.

PART II.

WATER—COSMETICS—DIET—SLEEP— REMEDIES.

THE complexion is one of the points that are noticed first in a woman's appearance. When good, it makes even the faultiest features pass muster. A clear complexion often runs in families, "like wooden legs. Though it is not invariably a token of good health, yet the best way to ensure it is to keep the body free from ailment. The bath is a valuable aid to the necessary purity of skin, but, like all beneficial processes, it is liable to abuse. The hot bath, especially, is misused to a great extent. It should never be taken very hot, for it then induces a weakened condition of the frame, which cannot fail to be at least temporarily injurious. I know several people who habitually indulge in two or three hot baths every week. After

To ensure a good complexion.

Good and ill effects of the bath.

these baths the complexion is always at its best, but ultimately it must suffer from the ever-recurring weakened condition of the body. A warm bath, as distinct from a hot one, is seldom injurious, but the safest are the tepid or the quite cold. No one **A simple test.** should begin these last quite late in life, unless the constitution is an unusually vigorous one. The test is a simple one. If, after the bath, when the skin is dried, the whole surface of the body glows with heat and is suffused with a pink tint, all is well. But if this reactionary warmth fails to respond to vigorous rubbing with the towels the bath is injurious. A chill often follows the hot bath, which proves how dangerous it is. If a chill follows the cold bath it must be abandoned at once and the tepid tried. Much depends upon the circulation, whether it be brisk or sluggish. If the former, the cold bath may almost certainly be ventured upon with uniformity, and become a daily delight. But if the circulation be slow and defective, a large can of hot water must be added to the cold. Only a short time should be allowed to the bath proper, whether hot, warm, tepid or cold ; but the drying process must be thorough and vigorous.

A good way of applying to the face all the beneficial effects of the hot bath without taking one and thus weakening the body. is by using a vaporiser, a neat

and ingenious little apparatus by means
of which the skin may be steamed
with great ease and even
pleasure. It consists of a
tiny nickel-plated kettle, set
in the top of a black cage,
and provided with a metal funnel
and a removable glass one. Under
the kettle is a small spirit lamp, also
protected by the cage. This provides
the heat needed to boil the water
in the kettle, and when steam is
produced the glass funnel conveys
it in a cloud upon any part of the face
to which it may be directed. It has
been found useful in shaving, as its
action softens the beard. Nor does its
utility end here. It has been found
invaluable for the self-administration
of spray remedies for such maladies as
affect the throat, lungs, mouth, eyes
and ears. Dr. Startin, the great
authority on skin diseases, recommends it highly.

A good substitute for the hot bath.

A bag of bran in the bath softens the
skin of the bather.

It is an excellent plan, when dressing
for dinner, to wash the face in water as
hot as the hands can bear.
It is not only delightfully
refreshing, but it clears the
pores of the skin more effectually than
cold or tepid water, and it often prevents a disagreeable flushing of the face
likely to come on in the warm dining-
room. More particularly is it advisable
after one has been out driving or walking

Hot water for the face.

in the cold wind, or in frosty weather. When feeling very tired I have often found the very, hot water extremely refreshing, and just the thing needed to give me the energy to dress after a tiring day's work.

During life the skin is continually undergoing the processes of reproduction and decay, by **Necessity for Cleanliness.** which the cuticle, or outer skin, is being constantly thrown off in the shape of minute scales or dust. This, mingling with the oily and aqueous matter of the perspiration, acquires sufficient adhesiveness to attach itself to the surface of the body. Unless the accumulation be daily removed by friction and washing, the channels of the perspiration become choked, and the functions of the skin, as a respiratory organ, are interfered with or suspended. The hair, too, becomes loaded with scurf and dust, and the pores of the skin under it choked with the exuviæ before referred to, by which the hair bulbs are strangled ; the teeth accumulate organic matter in their interstices, and the enamel is encrusted with animalculæ.

The principal recipe for the preservation and promotion of health and beauty, therefore, is thorough **The prime recipe.** cleanliness, which maintains the skin in its softness, the complexion in its natural hue, and the frame in vigour.

THE COMPLEXION.

Extreme pallor of the skin generally arises from debility, from languid circulation of the blood at the surface of the body, or from want of out-door exercise.

Treatment for pallor.

The main treatment consists of warm baths, frictions, and stimulating lotions.

Bathing is beautifying ; true. But there is an art in bathing, as in everything else, whether it is undertaken in the open sea or in the bathroom. A very hot bath is extremely exhausting to most persons, and should very seldom be indulged in.

Bathing an art.

After having washed the body all over in cold or tepid water, dress warmly, and walk for an hour at least ; exercise is essential to health, without which beauty cannot exist, and this is an important item in preserving one's looks.

Exercise essential to health.

The fresh water stimulates the blood, and gives, naturally, that rosy tint to the complexion which it is the aim of all cosmetics to impart. The exercise, shaking off the lassitude caused by fatigue, gives a steady circulation to the blood which enables it to flow freely through the natural channels, and imparts to the skin the fresh colour which is such a charm in women.

When very tired, sponge the face with soft, hot water, a very little good soap, and a drop or two of glycerine. Lather the face with this, rinse it off, and dry the skin with oatmeal. Then wash the meal off with clean, hot water, and spray cold water over the face till the skin is firm. Dry it gently, and put a little fullers' earth on.

A hint for tired people.

There is a refinement of cleanliness which is rarely understood. How many girls, for instance, know how to wash their faces ? Comparatively few. This may seem too absurd an assertion to be accepted for a moment. Well ! Let us see.

The face is more exposed to the dust and soil of daily life than any other part of the frame. The hands are gloved when we go out, but the face is unprotected, save by a thin veil, which very often rather adds to the evil of dirt than averts it. Consequently, the face needs more washing than even the hands. And this is how it should be done. The water must not be quite cold in winter, and soap should be used but once a day. The fingers are better than any sponge or glove or flannel, and they should be used as the masseuse uses hers, pressing them firmly but gently into the skin, and passing them two or three times over every inch of the face. More particular pains should be devoted to the corners, where dust is always liable to lodge, round the eyes, nose, and mouth. If a towel is used it should be of the softest and finest, and plenty of water must be applied after the soap,

How to wash the face.

so as to wash it all away. The drying process should be equally thorough and effectual, a hurried rub opening the way to all sorts of roughnesses and chappings. It is literally true that not one girl in twenty knows how to wash her face, and this is why massage flourishes so much. It thoroughly cleanses.

I will guarantee a good complexion to any healthy girl who will wash her face as described above, every night and morning, and at least twice additionally every day.

It is an excellent plan to rub a silk handkerchief gently but steadily over the face after washing it. This will serve to dry it thoroughly, and will also give that polish (without shininess) to the skin that Nature intended it to have. The forehead is particularly improved by this treatment.

An inexpensive beautifier.

The life of the skin is the natural oil which nature stores up under it, and supplies to the surface as required. Until we are twenty-five we have a sufficient supply of the oil. But it grows less and less as we advance in years, and after thirty nature needs assistance if we wish to preserve our freshness. The over-heated, dry atmosphere of our rooms does more to exhaust the oil supply than anything else. If we allow the supply of oil to get too low the skin shrivels, the muscles relax, and we get flabby and hollow-cheeked.

On the contrary, by feeding the skin with the proper oils we can preserve **Assisting nature.** the firmness of the flesh and the roundness and plumpness of the face almost indefinitely. Even if a person is sick and becomes thin and emaciated, she need not show it in the face.

It is injurious to the pores of the skin to be clogged with powder, creams, and rouge of any description, but often young and pretty women cover their faces with all sorts of sticky stuff, unrealising the Nemesis **The aftermath of cosmetics.** that awaits them in the future. After a few years of cosmetics, the skin becomes raddled and coarse, and the natural complexion, however perfect it may have been in the commencement, is utterly ruined. Extraordinary as it may appear, the loveliest complexions are frequently touched up in this silly—fatuously silly—way. Painting the rose and gilding refined gold would be equally absurd. But the idea would seem to be that Art is superior to Nature. The ruinous results may be seen on many an elderly face, to which the ravages of cosmetics have imparted an almost disreputable appearance. As a girl once remarked of another girl's painted and dyed old mother, "I should never take her out if she were mine!" After a long course of making-up it is impossible to continue it on moderate lines. It becomes a mockery, a burlesque, an extravaganza, and if some kind fairy would only allow the votaries of cosmetics to see themselves as others see them, there would be an end of make-up for many a long year. A touch of rouge is sometimes a great embellishment, but fatal, invariably fatal, to true good looks is the constant use of it.

Moderation impossible.

Sea breezes are marvellous rejuvenators, where there is some little remnant of youth to work upon; but without a portion of the original material, effort is thrown away. The complexions that are bought in the shops at so much the box have to be very careful when sea breezes are about. By the way, there has been a pretty little story going about at a certain watering-place not unknown to English visitors, about one of those ladies who take to pieces, so to speak. She was obliged, in a case of great crush at her hotel, to share her room for one night only with a small but precocious and extremely dangerous little niece. When the artificial aunt retired for the night, she carefully placed an impromptu screen between the bed and the dressing-table, by means of spreading out a travelling rug and pinning one end of it to the bed-curtains, and tying the other to the bed post. This performance must

Sea breezes and the complexion.

have awakened the small intruder, for
after her aunt had taken off nearly all
her hair, carefully washed off her
complexion, and placed her teeth in
a tumbler of water, a voice remarked,
with some disappointment in its tone,
"Aren't you going to take your eyes
out?" The owner of the voice had
crept out of the bed on the further side,
and had seated herself on the floor to
see if there was anything amusing
going on. She bewailed her disappointment all over the hotel next
morning. A nice little niece is charming; but a dreadful child like this is a
terror to evildoers.

If people who regularly use powder
could only realise how destructive the
practice is to the skin, and how exceedingly nasty the results are, they
would gladly try what radiant, perfect
cleanliness would do. Several guineas'
worth of rouge and powder
Pure water the best cosmetic. can be outdone by a plen-
tiful use of pure water,
if only sensibly applied.
There is now in England a lady who
is acknowledged to be beautiful. As
a girl she was absolutely plain, or as
plain as any girl could be with fine
eyes and abundant hair. As she grew
up, her mother applied all sorts of
creams and washes to her skin, and
confided the care of her hair to the
best artists in that line. One day the
girl, looking at herself in the glass,
resolved that she would use no more

of the horrid little messes that were
for ever being laid on or rubbed into
her skin. She had noticed the black-
ness of the water in which her face
had been washed free of all these
costly impurities, preparatory to a
further application. "If I can't be
pretty, at least I will be clean," she
told her mother. She made a fine art
of cleanliness. Her skin
The reward of simplicity. grew clearer, softer, more
pearly every week. Her
masses of hair, which used to be
clogged with dyes, developed lovely
tones of bronze and brown and gold.
Her eyes, set in a complexion of
milky transparence, shone liquid, large
and clear. The eyebrows, brushed
regularly, lost their tendency to be
unduly thick and rampant near the
nose, and meagre at the temples.
Their splendid arch is now one of the
striking features in a charming face.
The lips grew healthily red, and
plenty of fresh air and exercise imparted, among other good things, the
crowning beauty of ever-varying soft,
bright tinting, which no one could ever
mistake for an instant for the fixed
colour produced by artificial means.

Why are so many busy women
haggard and wan, bereft of their
pristine, clear complexions and of the
good looks with which they
A word to clever women. began their work in life?
Because, clever as they may
be, they are deficient in common-sense,

33

and suffer internally as well as externally in consequence. The women who pursue callings in which education and a certain amount of culture are necessary, suffer many things from the lack of this common-sense. The odd thing is that they can often use it with regard to others, while they absolutely ignore it in their own case. They can preach sound gospel to each other, but with regard to themselves nothing appears to be " worth while." A sort of very genuine humility lies at the root of much of this, but there is also an alloy of indolence occasionally that is very reprehensible.

Women who work at journalism, teaching, or secretarial tasks know only too well the feeling **A serious mistake.** of " dead-beatness " with which they return to solitary lodgings, longing for food, but too tired to take any trouble to get it. Busy landladies cannot be expected to wait on them at all hours, and maidservants in lodgings have usually plenty to do. So the poor brainworker sits down, worn out with fatigue, and often falls asleep, foodless, in pure exhaustion, only to wake unrefreshed, and even more prostrate with fatigue than before. This is one of the numerous fatal things **Sharing rooms.** to which women give way when there is no one but themselves to consider. That is why the " chum " system is ever so much better than to live alone. However tired one is, there is some inducement to make things bright and cheery and to prepare a tempting meal when there are two to benefit by one's exertions, and when a voice is expected to say by and by, "Oh, how good of you! How jolly everything looks! It's quite reviving!"

Miss Louisa Alcott left her delightful work and the world long before she need have done so, but **Miss Alcott.** she had drawn such huge draughts upon her own energies that when the bills came to be met she found herself insolvent! Her energies had been overworked, and could not answer to the call. Fuel, in the shape of nutritious and regular food, had been denied when most needed by the mental machinery and the physical force, without which the clearest brain cannot work. And the result? Premature death to the gifted, and the loss to the world of how many successors to such inestimably valuable books as "Little Women" and "Good Wives." The story told in her letters and journals contains a lesson that every hard-working woman should lay to heart.

She writes, January, 1874: "When I had the youth I had no money; now **"The pace that kills."** I have the money I have no time, and when I get the time, if ever I do, I shall have no health to enjoy life." Hers was a noble task, self-imposed, that of clearing her family of debt, "sending sister to Italy and keeping the old folks cosy." She did it all, brave heart! and "made haste to be rich" for the most unselfish purposes.

If she had only remembered that "it's the pace that kills." One cannot but suspect that the family laid far more on her, in other ways **Family selfishness.** besides money-earning, than they should have done. That is almost always the way when there is one capable member. The others bring their burdens, great and small, and add them to what has to be borne by the one whose energies are always active and respond to every demand.

Young women seem to imagine that youth and health will last for ever, and they play sad tricks with their digestion, sometimes going **Abusing one's** without food for hours to-**constitution.** gether, sometimes offering their splendid appetite the moult of a penny bun, instead of the good mid-day meal it expects and deserves. The wonder is that so few people generally die of neuralgia and meningitis when they lay themselves out to invite these dispensations. Women abuse themselves and their own constitutions frightfully, and they do not know it.

Do let us take the lesson to heart. Good food is a good investment. It

36

will improve the quality of our work and add to its quantity. Let us reform, before it is too late, and leave our evil ways of tea and toast, buns and milk, eluding dinner and evading supper when there is no one but ourselves to profit by outlay and exertion. We shall be more capable, more amiable, and ever so much better looking in consequence.

Sound and refreshing sleep has a most beneficial effect upon the complexion. The habit of falling asleep at a few moments' notice is **Sleep a great beautifier.** one to be encouraged in the interests of health, a more important consideration than that of mere colouring, but one which is inextricably bound up with it. After unusual fatigue, the face of even a young woman has a drawn and tired look which ages it palpably. Even a quarter of an hour's sound sleep removes this and replaces it by the soft commingling of white and palest pink which is the characteristic of the finest blonde complexions, or the rose and olive of the brunette.

Arsenic has been used for improving the complexion, doses of the poison having been regularly swal- **A dangerous remedy.** lowed with this aim. The girl or woman who would wilfully impregnate her system with a dangerous drug, merely in order to look nice, could never *be* nice. She certainly is not mentioned in the thirtieth chapter of Proverbs. Her husband's heart could hardly trust in her, and her children would already have lost their childish faith in their mother before they were old enough to know anything about her toilet devices.

Diet has a great effect upon the complexion. Simple food, as varied as possible and cooked to perfection, is good for both health and looks. Rich sauces, highly seasoned dishes, and several different kinds of wine at dinner, play havoc with the pink and white of even fresh young cheeks. Could anything be less poetic than a pimple ? Yet this is what happens if the above complicated dietary be followed. Edwin does not like the look of a pimple on his wife's face, and she detests herself whenever she sees it in the glass. Simple dishes eaten with enjoyment and digested merrily, not sadly and moodily, bring brightness to the eyes and freshness to the cheeks. Most of us eat too much meat and not enough vegetable and fruit.

Exercise is an important factor in the matter, and even dress has something to do with it. Many a busy, thrifty woman, who spends the morning hours in happily looking after her home, trotting upstairs to the linen cupboard, downstairs with sheets to mark or mend, up again to put them away into the bath-room, and generally all over

The importance of diet.

Insufficiency of domestic exercise.

the place, being on foot for a couple of hours or more, is under the impression that she has had quite the right thing in the shape of exercise. By no means. She has had no fresh air, no change of scene, no fresh sources of thought. It is these things that make open-air exercise so necessary. The mind is invigorated and refreshed as well as the muscles.

Veils do more to ruin the complexion than any other thing. The skin needs the friction of the air. Constant covering interferes with the circulation and the healthy action of the pores. It heats the face, and keeps it covered with an oily moisture, which catches the dust and dirt and gets into the pores. Often poisons used in the dye of the veil have injurious effects. When the face is left exposed the air blows off the dust and keeps the skin dry and clean. It also stimulates the circulation and gives colour to the cheeks.

On veils.

"Acne," or black spots, are frequently observed on the skin in hot weather, particularly on the face. These are formed by the accumulation of the indurated solid matter of the perspiration in its pores. It is a common practice to force them out by pressure of the fingers, but that causes a slight swelling, and they are more successfully removed by the use of vapour-baths, and friction, assisted by a mild lotion which prevents their re-forming.

Cure of Acne.

For banishing black spots, an excellent ointment is made of flowers of sulphur, one teaspoonful ; rose-water, one pint ; glycerine, one teaspoonful. If the specks are very obstinate and hard to remove this preparation should be used : Liquid ammonia, twenty drops; ether, one drachm ; soft soap, one ounce. Bathe the place affected with hot water and then rub in a little of this mixture with the ball of the thumb. Then wash it off with hot water. Here is another remedy for black spots :

An excellent ointment.

Dilute a tablespoonful of gin with two tablespoonfuls of cold water. Wash the face regularly with this night and morning, mixing it fresh each time.

Another remedy.

Acne is caused originally by neglect of cleanliness, which does more than anything else to ruin the skin and complexion.

Tea and coffee should be avoided, and cocoa and warm milk substituted for them. Do not eat pastry, sauces, cheese, or any highly seasoned dishes, but you cannot eat too freely of fruit, tomatoes, and well-cooked green vegetables. At night wash the face in hot water and steam it well, rubbing a little good eau-de-Cologne into the skin. Never use face powder.

Diet for acne.

A doctor says : " Eat fruit for breakfast. Eat fruit for luncheon. Avoid pastry. Shun muffins and crumpets and buttered toast. Eat whole-meal bread. Decline potatoes if they are served more than once

Advice worth following. a day. Do not drink tea or coffee. · Walk four miles every day. Take a bath every day. Wash the face every night in warm water, and sleep eight hours. You will never then need nerve medicines." Nor will cosmetics be needed, unless there happens to be something radically wrong with the constitution. And may I add to the above recommendation : " Do something kind for some one at least once a day. Never give way to irritability, but practise per-

A new recipe for rosy cheeks. fect control over the temper." Bad temper affects the liver and the liver affects the complexion. Happiness and kind-heartedness, if allowed to result in good-natured actions, bring roses to the cheeks, brightness to the eyes, and smoothness to the brow.

Two American doctors who collaborated in writing a book on digestion say about bread : " Bread

The staff of life. is verily the staff of life, if rightly baked ; if not, it is a broken reed." My own opinion about bread is that it should never be eaten when " slack-baked," as the bakers call it, and I fancy that this is what the above advice comes to. " Rightly baked " must mean thoroughly baked. If any one has ever examined the usual contents of a baker's barrow he will see two dozen pallid and half-baked loaves to every half-dozen that are really brown and crusty. But those who desire to avoid indigestion should insist on having all their bread well baked. If this is persisted in there will be a little difficulty at first, but after a while the baker will become accustomed to the order, and will even bake loaves specially for such customers as insist upon crusty ones and decline to take any others.

America is a great country for sweets, there usually called candy. **Sugar.** But this is what the above-quoted doctors say : " Sugar is pure fuel with no waste matter, and every particle must be burned up in the system." When too much sugar is consumed it prevents the burning up of other food, and this leads to serious consequences. Not too many sweets, please, girls !

They do not put at all too fine a point upon it about pickles. This is **Pickles.** what they say : " Pickles are the enemy of the human race. There is absolutely nothing that can be said in favour of them. There is something peculiar and abnormal in the craving for them, and this is especially true of school children, who, of all persons, ought to be the last to eat them."

Many a girl owes ill-health and a miserable complexion to an undue fondness for vinegar. The healthy appetite rarely asks for it. The craving increases by indulgence, and the result is a sallow skin, painful thinness, and nervous ailments.

Vinegar and health.

Freckles trouble many a girl. I used to be told, when I was a girl, and objected to freckles on my own nose, that they were considered a beauty. To say that I accepted the statement with a grain of salt would be a very inadequate way of expressing my sentiments. A whole salt mine would not have sufficed to induce me to receive it as truth. Freckles are far from pretty. And when the nose is red as well there is considerable reason for a girl to be discontented with her looks. If your nose is red look to your digestion, or the tightness of your corsets. If it freckles easily apply a freckle lotion. With the shape of the nose you may not tamper with impunity, but its complexion may be improved. If the nose is chronically red, either the digestion is impaired, or tight lacing is responsible. Diet and exercise will cure the one, and commonsense the other. At the end of this chapter will be found some practical advice on the getting rid of freckles.

About freckles.

An orange eaten first thing in the morning, followed by a glass of hot water, sipped slowly, is good for both liver and complexion.

For the complexion.

Wash the face with a lather of good soap and warm, soft water every night before retiring. Then rinse **To get a good complexion.** it with rain-water if possible —if not, with warm water; spread toilet oatmeal over the wet face, and massage gently till the skin glows. Then rub in the cold-cream mentioned at the end of this chapter for ten minutes. This only applies to a naturally dry skin.

For pimples on the face the following lotion is recommended by an authority: To 5 oz. of elder- **To remove pimples.** flower water add 1 oz. of spirits of camphor, and one drachm of milk of sulphur. Shake thoroughly. Wash the face at night with tepid water and soap, and after drying the face apply the lotion with a soft sponge or a puff of cotton; let the lotion dry on.

Rub the face over just before washing it with two teaspoonfuls of flower of sulphur mixed in half a pint **To clear the complexion.** of new milk. This mixture should stand awhile first.

Doctors say that apples act directly upon the liver, thus strengthening the digestion, and, as a conse- **The apple as a beautifier.** quence, improving the texture of the skin and the tints of the complexion. Raw apples are the best, but baked ones may be substituted for a change, or if the fresh fruit should be found unpalatable or difficult of digestion. The old rule that fruit in the morning is gold, in the afternoon is silver, and in the evening is lead, is quite exploded. Many people find that a light meal of ripe fruit directly before getting into bed induces comfortable sleep, and in every way is an immense success.

Every one should make it a practice to eat an orange or an apple before going to bed. A raw onion is said to have the same beneficial effect upon the health and therefore upon the looks, but there are other results not so agreeable, which every person of refinement would avoid. Prunes are excellent, when apples and oranges are unattainable.

Fruit at night.

Too much passivity of disposition deprives the countenance of the charm of mobility. To be always smiling makes wrinkles as surely as to be always frowning ; and a chronic smile becomes eventually unattractive, however white and perfect may be the teeth it shows, however charming the curve of the lips.

Of wrinkles.

The old days of " prunes and prisms," with many other of the old beauty maxims, have passed away. Women are no longer afraid to smile often for fear of producing wrinkles. A passive, emotionless life is not now considered conducive to good looks. On the contrary, people who feel vividly are those who look young longest.

"Calm's not youth's crown."

They do not suffer from the trick of the mannered smile that so often leaves an impress of artificiality, and even insincerity, on the countenance, to say nothing of its wrinkles on the skin. More impressible natures, with their quick alternations of mood, their ready laughter, their sympathy in the joys and sorrows of others, their deeply-felt loves and friendships, write such a changing, fleeting, ever-varying record on the face that wrinkles have no time to carve themselves. It is the fixed simper, the constant frown, the sour and fretted peevishness, that bring them out too soon. Sometimes heavy cares and deep grief are responsible, but with them they often write indelibly upon the countenance the evidence of a beauty of character that trials, nobly borne, have ineffaceably indited.

The chin should be round, white, and well-modelled. Resolution and firmness are expressed by a well-formed chin, while weakness of disposition is shown in a retreating one. The author of a work on noses says that we may, in a very appreciable degree, form our own noses, and it is at least equally true that we can do much towards securing well-formed chins. If circumstances favour the development of firmness in character, the chin improves steadily under those circumstances. If, on the contrary, weakness and irresolution, and a tendency to be easily led by others,

The chin.

become fixed in the nature and fostered by events, the chin retreats more and more in consonance with the deterioration of the will. Balzac says: " La vie habituelle fait l'âme et l'âme fait la physiognomie."

Every time we think a kindly thought of others, or entertain a generous purpose, a line of **Character and countenance.** sweetness and goodness comes into the face, and with repetition soon becomes engraven there. Daily difficulties overcome without grumbling or despondency, daily duties performed ungrudgingly and conscientiously, all write themselves on our countenances, producing that look of integrity and honesty that makes others trust us when we deserve that they should.

And self-denial does its part **Self-denial.** towards making the expression sweet and good ; but self-denial should never degenerate into that officious putting of others before ourselves which engenders selfishness in those about us and self-righteousness in those who practise it ! I think it is Austin Dobson who sings, àpropos to refusing alms to those we meet—

" Always our hearts to be hardening thus,
If good for the beggars, is bad for us."

And the converse is true. If we are always victimising ourselves for the sake of others it may possibly be good for us, but it is very certainly bad for them. So we must not be selfishly unselfish, but leave a chance or two to others to practise the same virtue.

The care of our teeth and hands may be considered as forming part of our duty to our neighbour, as well as to ourselves. The aspect of untended teeth is extremely disgusting, and that of uncared-for finger-nails almost equally so. White teeth give a decided charm to the countenance, and would in this matter repay any trouble expended upon brushing them, even if this did not, as virtue is said to do in the proverb, bring its own reward. The delicious sensation of purity induced by the vigorous use of a rather hard tooth-brush is sufficient to induce the laziest to overcome their special failing. Most of us, however, who have any claim to the title of gentlewomen, do not neglect the daily cleansing, though only a small minority do their whole duty to these useful servants by cleaning them after every meal, as well as each morning and at night. It is really necessary to do this in order to keep them in perfect condition and avoid the toothache. Periodical visits should be made to the dentist for purposes of prevention, which is so much superior to cure, and so much less disagreeable where the teeth are concerned. Prevention is better than extraction, to alter the wise

The details of the toilet.

old proverb, and the skilled eye soon perceives something wrong and as quickly sets it right.

"Sweet as orris in Mass-time," says Browning, speaking of Florentine ladies, who love to keep a bit of the fragrant root in their mouths. Red and firm gums are great aids by contrast to the beauty of the teeth. Myrrh and alum both act beneficially on the gums. The teeth should be of the purest whiteness, and have a kind of clear look in them, like pebbles under water. They should be perfectly even, small in a woman, larger in a man. The upper teeth should protrude slightly over the under, but not in any pronounced degree.

The teeth.

A tincture that restores soundness to the gums is one ounce of coarsely-powdered Peruvian bark, steeped for a fortnight in half a pint of brandy. The mouth should be well washed night and morning with this mixture, diluted in an equal quantity of rose-water.

For the gums.

There is often a formation of tartar upon the teeth. For removing this incrustation Dr. Scoffern recommends muriatic acid or spirit of salt, strong, as obtained from the druggist. He says: "The name of the liquid will sound frightful enough to a timid girl, but if employed in the way to be described no ill effects will follow. The method of using is this: Procure a clean

To remove tartar.

skewer, one of those used by butchers,
hammer or batter out the sharp point
of it into a very small brush, not larger
than one of the small sable brushes
used in miniature painting. Dip this
into muriatic acid, allowing all superfluous acid to drain off, and rub the
part of the tooth to be purified. There
are very few incrustations which will
resist this treatment. Care should be
taken that, so soon as the operation is
finished, all lingering traces of the acid
be well removed from the mouth with
chalk and water ; afterwards with water
alone." For some time after the operation just described has been performed
the teeth will feel rough, will "be set
on edge," to use a common expression,
a sufficient indication of *the destruction
which must result from habitual recourse
to the process.*

Camphorated chalk is a safe dentifrice, and gives a delightful sensation
of purity to the mouth. A
very pleasant dentifrice is
made with an ounce of finely-
powdered green sage, mixed in a tablespoonful of white honey. A preparation for decaying teeth is composed of
two scruples of finely powdered myrrh,
a scruple of juniper gum, and ten grains
of rock alum, mixed in honey.

A safe
dentifrice.

In childhood the teeth should be
most carefully attended to. When the
second teeth are coming, they should
be watched so that, on the first appearance of a tendency to irregularity, the

child should be taken to a clever dentist.

To artificial teeth no one can make any objection, so important are they to the general health when the **Artificial teeth.** natural teeth have fallen out. When these become necessary, the greatest care should be taken to find out a really reliable dentist.

Miss Frances Power Cobbe admits there is no harm in artificial teeth where "no deception" is meant, and where the object is to supply a want, not "to forge a claim to beauty." That this latter consideration has no influence in the matter is a question that may be left entirely to the inner consciousness of the wearers of false teeth. Miss Cobbe thus sums **Tokens of health.** up the tokens of health : "Clear eyes, clear skin, rich hair, good teeth, a cool, soft hand, breath like a bunch of cowslips, and a free and joyous carriage of the head and limbs."

A FEW BEAUTY DON'TS.

Don't go out in blustery weather without a veil unless you wish a tanned skin or freckles. **A few Beauty Don'ts.** March winds are proverbial for giving the skin an old, leather-like appearance, and every woman knows how next to impossible it is to remove freckles.

Don't forget when drying the face

after washing to rub upward toward the nose. This will prevent wrinkles and help smooth out to a great extent the crease alongside the nose.

Don't use either hot or cold water for bathing exclusively. A good rule to follow is a hot bath at night and a cold one in the morning.

Don't wear tight shoes if you desire a graceful carriage; no woman can walk comfortably or well in a shoe that is too small. Besides, a small shoe distorts the foot in an unnatural manner that deceives no one.

Don't depend entirely on soap and water for cleaning the hands. Have a small brush to scrub them, a cake of pumice-stone—the velvet kind—to remove stains, and some borax to whiten them.

Don't resort to artificial means to furnish what nature has denied you. Powder clogs the pores of the skin and rouge is only fit to be used behind the footlights. Moreover, it is not an improvement; nothing is pretty that is not natural.

Don't cut the skin at the base of the nails with the scissors. An inexperienced hand is apt to do more harm than good. Have an orange-wood stick and just push it down gently when it is soft after washing the hands.

Don't fail to rub the scalp with the finger tips and then brush the hair vigorously every night. This will keep the hair soft and glossy, help remove the dandruff (particles of dead skin that rub off when the scalp is too dry), and obviate to a certain extent the tendency to get grey, for when the hair and scalp are in good, healthy condition, the hair retains its colour longer.

Don't attribute the desire to preserve one's physical charms to personal vanity. The first element of beauty is health, and she who would be beautiful must have pure blood and be sound of mind and healthy of body.

USEFUL RECIPES.

One tablespoonful of prepared Californian borax, an ounce of precipitated chalk, half an ounce powdered orris-root, one drachm rose pink. Mix well together by aid of pestle and mortar. A most fragrant and pleasant preservative for the teeth and sweetener of the breath.

An excellent tooth-powder.

The best mouth washes may be bought in tablet form. Two of them can be made into a wash that will last a week. Orris-root tablets are excellent, imparting the fragrance of violets. Keep the teeth scrupulously clean, and at the slightest hint of decay go at once to the dentist—the best one that can be found.

Mouth Washes.

Dissolve a tablespoonful of prepared Californian borax in a pint of hot water; before the water is quite cold add a teaspoonful of spirits

A good mouth wash.

of camphor and one teaspoonful of tincture of myrrh.

A wineglassful or more should be used night and morning, or at any other time.

Add a tablespoonful of prepared borax and a drachm of camphor to a bottle or decanter containing

Another mouth wash.

about a pint and a half of cold or warm water. The clear liquid can be used as found agreeable, and more water added as required, until all the borax and camphor are dissolved. The excess of camphor will float on the top and excess of borax fall to the bottom, to be taken up as fresh water is supplied.

"Myrrh and borax" is a splendid preparation for the teeth; if regularly used it hardens the gums

Simple dentifrices.

and prevents looseness of the teeth. Orris also makes a pleasant dentifrice. Sage is unrivalled for the teeth.

For sun scorching, after boating or bathing, wash your face in water as hot as you can bear it, with

Sun-scorched faces.

some extract of elder-flowers in it, or a dessertspoonful of the best glycerine.

To soften toilet water, throw as much borax as can be heaped on a shilling into the jug, or the contents

Borax for the toilet water.

of a whole penny packet of boraxaline should be put in

the water jug at night; the water will be beautifully soft in the morning.

Its beneficent action on the skin makes it effective in removing freckles, blotches, and rough patches, due to an unhealthy condition of the pores. A solution of prepared borax, used daily, will restore the healthy tone, and make the skin soft, white, and effective.

A systematic use of a solution for the teeth preserves the dental organs, destroys tartar, and strengthens the gums. **For the teeth.**

Take half an ounce of alkanet and three ounces of oil of almonds; put these in an earthen vessel in a warm place to melt. In another vessel put an ounce and a half of white wax, and half an ounce of spermaceti; melt these also. When it is liquid add it to the oil, and put in twelve drops of otto of roses. Stir the mixture till it is thick, and put it in a cool place to get cold. **A lip salve.**

Cucumber peelings should be boiled in water, which should be kept for the toilet. A slice of cucumber may be rubbed on the face instead of soap. **Cucumber for the skin.**

Dill-water is as good for the complexion as rose-water; it makes the skin paler.

Elder-flower water is famous for its cooling properties, as is lavender.

Two ounces of orange-flower water; four ounces oil of almonds; half-ounce white wax; half-ounce spermaceti. Stand a jar containing these in a saucepan of hot water. **Home-made cold-cream.** Stir it well, adding the orange-flower water when the mixture is smooth. Mix all well, and keep it in an earthenware jar.

Cucumber, sliced, and soaked for a few hours in milk, is good for sunburn. **Cure for Sunburn.** Bathe the face two or three times a day with it. Dry the face very carefully, and on no account use a hard towel.

To remove freckles use the following : One ounce lemon juice ; quarter drachm powdered borax ; **To remove freckles.** half drachm pulverised sugar. Mix all, let it stand in glass for a few days, then apply it, and let it dry on the skin. Or : apply with a linen cloth two tablespoonfuls of grated horse-radish mixed with a teacupful of sour milk. The nose is very apt to freckle, even when no other parts of the face are affected in the same way. These little brown spots can be removed by putting on the nose a little of this lotion : Lemon juice, three ounces ; vinegar, one ounce ; rose-water, one ounce ; Jamaica rum, one ounce. Apply this with a sponge several times a day. When the face is washed care must be taken to dry the nose downward, not upward, and whenever the nose is touched with the hand or handkerchief, the same advice must be borne in mind, or very ugly results will follow.

CARE OF THE HAIR, EYES, EYE-LASHES, EYEBROWS, HANDS, AND FEET.

"That fawn-skin dappled hair of hers,
    And the blue eye,
    Clear and dewy,
And that infantine fresh air of hers."
      A Pretty Woman. BROWNING.

"His golden locks Time hath to silver turned ;
 O Time too swift, O swiftness never ceasing
 His youth 'gainst time and age hath ever
    spurned,
 But spurned in vain ; youth waneth by in-
    creasing.
 Beauty, strength, youth, are flowers but fading
    seen ;
 Duty, faith, love, are roots, and ever green."
             GEORGE PEELE.

"What grudge and grief our joys may then
    suppress
To see our hairs which yellow were as gold
Now grey as glass ; to feel and find them less,
To scrape the bald skull which was wont to
    hold
Our lovely locks with curling-sticks con-
    trouled,
To look in glass and spy Sir Wrinkle's chair
Set fast on fronts which erst were sleek and
    fair."
            GEORGE GASCOIGNE.

IT seems almost impossible to believe that in the middle of the nineteenth century hair oil of some kind

An odious custom.

or other was used by English-women of all classes of society, from the Queen down to the

57

little laundry-maid. So it was, however, and no toilet table was considered furnished without a pot of pomade. In Anthony Trollope's amusing little sketch "Crinoline and Macassar," he represents the lady as follows:—

> "With her hair done à l'Impératrice,
> Sweetly done with the best of grease."

On the next page, when the gentleman proposes marriage, this hair—"done with the best of grease"—is described as coming "in sweet contact" with his cheek.

Quite half the effect of one's appearance depends on successfully "doing the hair," and certainly half "Doing the hair." the trouble of the toilet is concerned with this process. When it is thick and of a pretty colour, and when the head is very well-shaped, the difficulty is but small. Whether the hair be "redolent ebony," or "the gold embrownment of a lion's eye," or "like gold-hued cloud-flakes on the rosy morn," or "silken locks of chestnut brown," if only they be abundant, the dressing is half done. But whatever be the tint, it cannot look its best unless well brushed and regularly washed.

The very best brushes should always be chosen, and if one has not a maid to use them vigorously upon Hair-brushes and one's locks, one must actively how use them in person, and administer at the very least one to use them. hundred strokes a day. The bristles

58

of the brushes should not be so hard as to drag the hair out by the roots in case of a tangle obstructing the brush's course. Nor should they be too yielding, as it is scarcely necessary to observe. It is useless to brush the hair unless the skin of the head be brushed as well. The friction stimulates it and makes the hair grow.

I have often seen girls brush their hair with slow and languid strokes which are simply useless. They might as well use the back of the brush. Vigour and intention are necessary to produce a really good effect, and induce the bright, healthy gloss that young hair should have.

I once heard a dark-haired girl say to a fair-haired one: "I would not have fair hair for the world. It has to be washed so often." That was an amazing speech. As though washing were only undertaken for appearance's sake! Dark hair needs it just as often as light. But I am really afraid that English girls do not wash their heads as often as they ought. It seems a dreadful thing to assert, and I should not venture to do so, had it not been a fashionable hairdresser who told me so. "Ladies neglect their hair," he said, "especially in the winter time." It certainly is a tremendous undertaking, to wash and dry long hair, but it is the only means of doing justice to Nature's ornamental frame for the face and protective clothing for the head. Once in every six weeks should the head be washed, and oftener in winter, when coal-fires make so much dust in even the best-kept houses.

The borax wash which I recommend is sold in packets by the Californian Pure Borax Co., each packet **Borax wash.** containing just sufficient for one washing. Plenty of warm water, free from lather, is needed after the process of cleansing has been gone through. The warm water should be poured over the head by a second person, the hair being held over a bath while this is being done. Yolk of egg makes an excellent wash for the hair, but even greater care is needed after its application than is the case with borax. Otherwise the hair will be sticky when dry. No time should be lost in drying the hair, otherwise a dangerous chill may be caught. The best way to dry it quickly and **To dry quickly.** thoroughly is after a good rub with dry towels, to sit on the rug in front of a good fire, and still rubbing, allow the heat to fall on the back, the sides and the top of the head alternately.

There ought to be a delightful glow after a good wash of the hair, and I have often fancied that this glow stimulates the brain. I suppose doctors would laugh at this idea, but it has been my experience again and again that thoughts flow freely and are fitted readily with phrases after abundant friction of the scalp.

I do not recommend the very common practice of having the hair shampooed **Shampooing.** at a hairdresser's shop. One nearly always catches cold after it, for the reason that it is impossible to get long hair thoroughly dried in a short time, and in its damp condition it has to be done up and so kept until the arrival at home. Far better let the shampooer attend at one's house. The fee is double, certainly, but the comfort and convenience and safety are well worth the difference.

A douche of cold water should always be poured over the head after those of warm water, and in cold **To guard against chills.** weather half a wineglassful of spirit, such as brandy, whiskey, rum or gin, should be rubbed well into the skin of the head to fortify it against a chill. Never do the hair up until it is perfectly dry, and shake it well about before beginning to brush and comb it after the bath. It feels just like feathers for a day or two, and is not easy to arrange, but that soon goes off.

Very often a good rubbing of the skin of the head serves to stimulate the growth of the hair. This **Treatment for thin hair.** ought to be repeated twice a week, and the friction should be so vigorous that the skin becomes red and glowing. Thin hair often becomes thick and long when this mode of treatment is applied to the head. Another useful experience for the hair is that of being allowed to float freely about for an hour or so, that the air may circulate through it.

The hair resembles a plant in some respects. Sunshine is good for it, and brings out the colour of brown or golden hair as nothing else can.

Baldness is annoying to a man, but it is horrible to a woman. Women are supposed to be the ornamental part of humanity, and even if not very liberally endowed with good looks, they ought to be pleasing to the sight in some respect or other. This is almost impossible where there is baldness. Not all the contrivances of all the wig-makers can provide an efficient substitute for the natural growth. The little top-knots that are sold under the name of " scalpettes " are seldom, if ever, successful in the part of deputy. They do not look at home with the other hair. It is the same with coils and curls that are arranged along the dressing-table and then pinned on the head. They have a sort of foreign look, and are readily detected to be strangers in a strange land.

All such artifices are to be avoided until every possible effort has been made to induce the hair to grow. There are some excellent preparations sold for this purpose. Others are much too greasy to commend themselves to the women of this day, who hold hair oil in abhorrence.

Sometimes false hair is worn when the natural crop is sufficiently abundant, to afford adequate material for a good coiffure, but the necessary skill is not forthcoming. It is well for a girl in such a case to take a few lessons in dressing her hair. A half-guinea is well spent in this way, for the effect of a good coiffure is surprisingly great.

Wearing false hair injures the natural growth by keeping the skin of the head too hot and thus impeding **Ill effects of false hair.** its functions and hindering its productiveness. Excessive use of the hot curling-tongs is injurious to the hair, rendering it dry and brittle. Once a week is as often as the tongs may be **Curling-tongs and pins.** used with impunity. Curling-pins are not calculated to injure the hair, even if used every night.

Grey hair is often very pretty, both in men and women. It must be thick, however, and really grey, not mixed with black or brown. A silvery grey is often quite lovely, whether brushed straight down after the commonplace fashion in which men " do " their hair, or piled high in snowy drifts on some elderly woman's head.

Cantharides makes an excellent hair-wash, when used in combination with certain other ingredients, but it is only useful when seldom and sparingly used. Oil of mace is a good stimulant, and holds no such risk as cantharides. It is generally used with spirits, such as whiskey, brandy, or rum, being well rubbed into the skin of the head. If it does not make it red and glowing, friction with a coarse towel or a piece of flannel should be applied. If all fails to make the skin red, no hair will grow, and further trouble is useless.

Stimulants for the hair.

In previous times there was nothing for it but either a wig or a false front. But the barbers of to-day supply us with all manner of useful and ornamental little additions, all of which may be seen illustrated in the pages of the journals for women's reading. There are no "toilet mysteries" nowadays. They are all advertised, explained, and pictorially elucidated in the pages of the weekly press.

No toilet mysteries to-day.

Hair-dyes are such a mistake, physiologically and artistically, that I have little else to say about them. I do not know if golden dyes injure the health, but I do know that those which turn the hair dark contain lead, which often results in mischief to the eyes, and, if persevered in, ends in paralysis. I have known of a few terrible cases of fatal illness following upon the persistent use of hair-dyes, after months of brain suffering of a most distressing

Dangerous hair-dyes.

kind. One case that came under my notice was so dreadful as to fill me with indignation against the people who can dare to prepare and sell these hair dyes, knowing well that they contain a deadly poison which slowly permeates the system, affects the brain, and ruins the health. I wish some of these conscienceless vendors could be prosecuted for manslaughter. They deserve severe punishment; for, though the people who use hair-dyes are often silly and blamable, they would not dream of applying them to their heads were they aware of the injurious ingredients they contain. Besides, there are people who dye their hair for the reason that an appearance of age would tell against them in their business or profession, and not from motives of vanity. Is it likely that they would willingly use a preparation adapted to rob them, after a few months, of the health and strength needed to pursue their avocation or calling?

It is sometimes possible to prevent the hair from turning grey, though impossible to make it brown or black again after the colour has once gone from it. After a long illness or a condition of low vitality from grief or depression, the hair often begins to turn grey in the prime of life. A good hairdresser should at once be consulted, and he can usually find some remedy.

To cut an inch or two from the ends occasionally helps in the restoration of the colour of the hair.

There is a great difference in the way the hair grows about the temples and ears. Sometimes it seems **Hints on arranging the hair.** to caress them prettily, curling round them in little rings and waves. Again, on some heads, the hair appears to shy away from the ears and avoid the temples, giving a bald kind of look to the face. Occasionally a little coaxing and contrivance may be found of use in persuading the hair to approach the cheeks and brow, but I have generally noticed that the women who are most disfigured by this sort of thing, do their best to make the most of it, brushing their hair back even further than its own inclination sends it. The back of such heads is a sad sight. The ears are left stranded with a wide beach between them and the hair, and a coil of the latter is so arranged as to make a hard, rigid line against the skin.

A small volume might be filled with remarks upon the arrangement of the hair. It is useless to expatiate upon the fashion of the day, since it changes so often and so radically that by the time these words appear in print there is no saying on what part of the head feminine the hair appertaining to it or purchased for it may be worn. A few general rules may not be unacceptable, however. With long faces, the hair should be kept flat on the top of the head, and allowed to be visible at the sides ; more especially should this be seen to when the forehead is narrow. High foreheads should be veiled with curls or fringes. Round faces need a visible edifice of hair upon the top of the head. Long necks forbid this arrangement, requiring some capillary furniture at the back. The catogan or *queue* style suits them best. This may occasionally be combined with a few high curls in front, but the effect of over-elaboration and of too great a weight of hair must always be carefully avoided. The best and most artistic styles are those which show the shape of the head under the arrangement of the hair ; that is one reason why the catogan style always takes so well whenever it is introduced. The classic knot at the back always looks well when the features are regular and the head finely formed. But then it is copied, with distracting results, by persons whose heads are out of drawing, and whose features match their heads.

A few general rules.

The fringe should never entirely conceal the forehead, unless, indeed, the dimensions of the latter are enormous. One of these paddock-like foreheads requires any amount of veiling. But in ordinary circumstances the fringe

Hints on fringes.

should be restrained from undue length and thickness, and should always be lifted in one part to show the brow. The ladies depicted in the old Books of Beauty understood this, and never committed the mistake of veiling the whole forehead with hair. It gives an animal look to the face.

No girl can be really plain who has good eyes and abundant hair, if she will only refrain from screwing up her locks into a displeasing tightness. With the hair, as with the face, ineffable cleanliness is a wonder - worker. "What lovely hair!" said a girl once, taking up a long, thick tress that lay on the glass counter in a barber's shop. A curious expression came into the man's face, as he replied, "It's your own, miss." She had grown that hair on her own head, but no one would ever have dreamed that what was on her own head at the moment had the smallest affinity with it. The dissevered tress was clean! In it were many shades of glossy brown, some like the rind of a horse chestnut, others with a tint of gold in them. The dull, dead, muddy brown of the hair under her hat needed only a touch from the magic wand of the fairy Cleanliness to be as beautiful.

Care of the hair.

The loveliest hair I ever saw belonged to a beautiful woman well-known in the highest circles of London society. That lovely hair lies low now, with the sweet grey eyes and the commanding beauty of the graceful figure.

A simple secret. "How do you keep your hair so bright in all this horrid London fog?" she was once asked, and replied that her brushes were never used twice without having been washed in the interval. Six of them lay on her toilet-table, and these were used in rotation. The inconvenience of frequently washing and drying such a quantity of hair, with the attendant risk of catching cold, was thus avoided. The method is a good one. Hair and brushes both get dusty, but if the latter are kept immaculately clean they do much to make and keep the former so.

The preparation of borax that is sold in packets on purpose for washing hair-brushes is excellent.

Washing hair-brushes. The water should be warm, but not boiling, when the contents of the packet are thrown into it. The brushes should be dabbed up and down in the water, and a thick lather will soon appear. The backs of the brushes should not be wet, and they must not be placed too near the fire to dry, or the varnish upon the wood will be injured. In the case of ivory-backed brushes, the ivory is likely to part and split if too much heat be applied.

Hair-dye is not only an error in eclecticism but an injury to good looks. The fashion is for every woman who

pretends to smartness to plaster on her
hair the pet dye of the moment,
whether it suits her colour-
Hair-dyes and ing or not. All the fashion-
individuality. able hair is then of exactly
the same tint. Could. anything be
more fatal to individual charm? If
every woman looked alike, how could
any man make choice? Why should
he fall in love with any individual
specimen? And yet the aim of
fashionable women seems to be to
look precisely like every other fashionable woman. There is a shade of red
that is astonishingly becoming to the
sort of complexion which the French
describe as "*mat*," but it makes pink
cheeks look vulgar and red ones
coarse. Yet there are women whose
cheeks are habitually pink and frequently red—not to say petunia—who
apply this dye to their hair.

Sometimes the hair turns grey while
the possessor is still young, and then
the temptation to dye it is
The strong, on account of the im-
possibilities pression of age conveyed
of grey hair. by grey hair. It should be
resisted, however, and the reward is
sometimes great. The natural colour
sometimes returns, and even if it
should not, there are great possibilities
of picturesqueness in grey hair. They
have been known to impart an aspect
of refinement to features that, with
hair of more vivid tinting, lacked
distinction. The softening effect is

observable in the expression of the eyes, and many a woman first discovered that she could be attractive when arrayed in powder costume for a fancy ball. Dyed hair goes but indifferently with wrinkled cheeks, especially when the dye chosen is of an infantine yellow tint. It usually is. One often sees babyish yellow curls surmounting an aged brow, and immediately thinks of the verse about grey hairs bringing honour. Dyed hairs bring ridicule !

For cleaning the hair and removing all scurf, dandruff, &c., dissolve a tablespoonful of prepared borax **Cleaning the hair.** in a pint of hot water, and wash the head with this solution, and use also a little soap ; then rinse with cold water, and dry the head well.

To a pint of hot water add a tablespoonful of prepared Californian borax, **Hair cream.** which will quickly dissolve ; then add one drachm of salts of tartar and one ounce of almond oil ; shake well and perfume, to suit the taste, with a few drops each of bergamot, lemon, lavender, and clove essential oils. A beautiful cream will be produced, which, shaken well before using, will impart a healthy gloss to the hair, purify the scalp, and act as a deterrent to the falling-off of weak and thin-grown hair.

Take rosemary herb with roots, two ounces, break it up into small pieces ;

borax, two tablespoonfuls ; place in a jug or other suitable vessel, and pour over a pint of boiling water ; cover the jug and let the contents steam near the fire for three hours, stirring occasionally. When cold, press out, pour off, and bottle the clear liquor, to which add one ounce of glycerine and shake well together. This makes an excellent preparation, removing scurf, dandruff, vermin, keeping the skin healthy and thus preventing baldness. It is far better than compounds containing alcohol and other irritants. If perfume is required, then add half a drachm each of bergamot, lemon, rose, and lavender. Any druggist will supply these at a small cost.

Rosemary hair restorer.

Soap and soda soften the bristles and will turn an ivory-backed brush yellow, so in case of the latter the following treatment is recommended : Rub plenty of flour well in, wrap the brushes up in paper and leave them all night ; in the morning give them a good shaking, and remove the remaining flour by blowing the brush. Ivory that has become yellow by age or usage may be whitened by a good rubbing with fine sand-paper or moist powdered pumice-stone.

To clean ivory backed brushes.

Tortoise-shell combs or ornaments that have lost their polish may be renovated by rubbing them with very finely powdered rotten-stone mixed with a little olive oil. The rotten-stone should be sifted through a piece of fine muslin before mixing **To renovate tortoise-shell combs.** it with the oil. When all marks are removed, polish them with jeweller's rouge and a soft chamois.

Always use scrupulously clean hair-brushes, and not a fine comb. Do not **To avoid dandruff.** wear anything which will heat the head, and be shampooed regularly. The following is recommended as a most excellent preventive of dandruff : Tincture of cantharides, one ounce ; Cologne, one ounce ; liquid ammonia, one drachm ; glycerine, half an ounce ; oil of thyme, and rosemary oil, half a drachm each ; mix altogether with six ounces of rose-water. Rub the scalp thoroughly with this preparation until no further evidences of dandruff are noticeable.

To keep the hair and scalp both in a healthy condition it is necessary that **Health of the hair.** they should be kept scrupulously clean. It is an erroneous idea to suppose that by washing alone this can be accomplished, for, if too often done, its effect is to make the hair rot and turn grey ; but at times it is required to remove dust or dirt. It is then advisable to dry it thoroughly and apply a softening wash.

The extreme length of some hair renders the process of washing it both troublesome and inconvenient. The use of a wash may be substituted with **Long hair.** advantage, and if followed by the patient and assiduous use of a good hair-brush, it will be found sufficient.

Hand brushing is calculated to promote the circulation in the vessels of the scalp when it is done **Hand brushing.** judiciously, that is gently, and with brushes the bristles of which are neither stiff nor closely set.

Science has made such a considerable advance of late in the treatment of the hair that no one need despair, and even in advanced cases of greyness, incipient or partial baldness, decay may be arrested and the hair restored to a healthy and luxuriant state. Immediate effects must not be anticipated, for such are not within the bounds of possibility ; but patience and perseverance will generally be rewarded by a satisfactory result.

Superfluous hairs, on the face or otherwise, are a cause of annoyance. Most depilatories, however, are **Superfluous hairs.** dangerous and only beneficial for a time.

Electrolysis is only applicable in the case of coarse hairs on the face. The process is quite out of the **Electrolysis.** question for the arms ; the roots lie too deep, as the electric needle is dug to the root of each hair.

Green tea used as a hair-wash darkens

it when it begins to lose colour. Condy's Fluid has a similar effect, but requires to be most carefully mixed, or the result will be streaky.

Green tea as a hair-wash.

Condy's Crimson Fluid is good for hair turning grey. Put half a wine-glassful in ten wineglassfuls of water, and wash the hair with it twice a week. This will be found to darken the colour of the hair almost imperceptibly.

To darken the hair.

A book published in 1645 says: "Take southernwood and burn it to ashes, and mix it with common oil; then anoint the bald place therewith morning and evening, and it will breed hair exceedingly."

An old recipe for the hair.

An ounce each of hartshorn, chloroform, and sweet almond oil, added to fifteen ounces of spirits of rosemary. Rub this well into the head, after a good brushing.

Sir Erasmus Wilson's recipe for falling hair and greyness.

Half ounce spirits of rosemary; the same of spirits of camphor, and half that of glycerine, the juice of a lemon; shake all well together, and then add four ounces of strong whiskey. Apply this every other night, alternating with a pomade composed thus: two ounces prepared lard, two drachms white wax; melt these gradually, then add four drachms of balsam of tolu, twenty drops of oil of rosemary, and two drachms of tinc-

For dry hair.

75

ture of cantharides. The balsam of tolu must be dissolved in half an ounce of rectified spirits of wine for twelve hours.

A few drops of hazeline in water is an excellent lotion for the eyelashes. **Long lashes.** They should be bathed in it every morning. A little powdered borax in water is also good, or even a still smaller quantity of carbonate of soda. But the best beautifier is healthy eyes. No one with weak eyes can expect to have long, thick lashes. Children should be taught not to rub the eyes, for this is most injurious to these sensitive organs. If a child has perfectly strong, healthy eyes, the lashes may be improved by occasionally slightly trimming them ; but this practice should be discontinued as one reaches maturer years, or no eyelashes will be the consequence.

Brushing the eyebrows and eyelashes every morning with a solution of green **For the eyebrows.** tea improves them. There is no better lotion for the eyes than salt water.

If the eyes are tired and burn, rest them, and bathe them in the following **For tired eyes.** simple yet excellent wash : To a quart of soft, boiled water add a tablespoonful of the best brandy and a teaspoonful of salt. Have the bedroom perfectly dark and do not place the bed in such a position that the early morning sunlight will shine in the eyes.

An excellent wash for red, tired eyelids is composed of one pennyworth of sulphate of zinc dissolved in a quart of water. The eyes should be bathed in a little of this twice daily and gently dried with a soft rag. I have known this wash cure obstinate cases of weak eyes.

Another recipe.

Smooth, glossy eyebrows and long, dark lashes add wonderfully to the beauty of a face, and women should care for these necessary adjuncts to their good looks. If the brows are thin and ill-formed rub pure grease or vaseline on them at night, bathing them carefully in cold water in the morning, and then putting on a little petroleum. Never brush or rub the brows the wrong way. Brush them daily with a small eyebrow brush that you can get at any good chemist's, but do not get into the habit of " rubbing " ; it will roughen and break the hairs.

Some beauty hints.

There is a great deal of character in the eyebrow. As the form and expression of the eyes and the regions about them have largely to do with feelings, pride, and self-control, the eyebrows are more particularly connected with the expression of those qualities or the reverse. When the eyebrows are ragged, unkempt, and scraggy, as we often see them, there is a lack of proper self-control. When they are straight and orderly, the reverse is the case.

Character in eyebrows.

If there is a tendency to pointed brows, with thinness of hair, there is an innate liking for display and vanity. When fluffy and extended deep on the nose, geniality and love are sure attributes. Light-tinged eyebrows show lack of ambition, while black brows indicate force, and the medium brown shade is indicative of coquetry.

An observant woman once wrote : Did you ever notice that men always instinctively put confidence in a girl with blue eyes, and have their suspicions of the girl with the brilliant black ones, and will you kindly tell me why ? Is it that the limpid blue eyes, transparent and gentle, suggest all the soft, womanly virtues, and because he thinks he can see through them, clear down into that blue-eyed girl's soul, that she is the kind of a girl he fancies she is ? I think it is, but some of the greatest little frauds I know are the purry, kitteny girls with big, innocent blue eyes.

Blazing black eyes, and the rich, warm colours which dark-skinned women have to wear suggest energy and brilliance and no end of intellect. Men look into such eyes and seem not to see below the surface.

They have not the pleasure of a long, deep gaze into immeasurable depths. And so they think her designing and clever, and perhaps (Save the mark!), even intellectual, when, perhaps, she has a wealth of love and devotion and heroism stored up behind that impulsive disposition and those dazzling black eyes, which would do and dare more in a minute for some man she had set that great heart of hers upon than your cold-blooded, tranquil blonde would do in forty years.

A mere question of pigment in the eye has settled many a man's fate in life, and established him with a wife who turned out very different from the girl he thought he was getting.

I read once, in an American paper, a refreshingly natural letter from some girls who wanted to be as pretty as possible. And what girl does not? "We will just love you if you will print something that will positively make the eyebrows grow, and that will also change the same from light golden to a darker shade that will not be very noticeable at first."

To be as pretty as possible.

I know that kind of girl, and that sort of sandy eyebrow with a flaxen gloss on it, so well. The girls want to be fitted out with all kinds of pretty finishing touches, but they do not want some of their acquaintances to say: "What have you been doing to darken your eyebrows?" and very likely add: "Do you think it an improvement?" in that exasperating tone of doubtful surprise in which so many disagreeable questions are asked. Those gleamy, glossy eyebrows are the despair of many a girl who cherishes her own ideal of what an eyebrow ought to be —a well-defined, narrow line of a tint just darker than the hair, and forming a feature in itself, adding depth and expression to the eye.

The following is the advice given in response to the request. The ingredients of the wash appear

A good eye-brow wash.

to be extremely well adapted to the purpose: Red vaseline, two ounces; tincture of cantharides, quarter of an ounce; oil of lavender, oil of rosemary, oil origanum, eight drops each. The eyebrows should be washed, well rinsed and dried before this lotion is applied. Get a small brush, resembling a tiny toothbrush, and, putting a little vaseline on it, carefully brush the eyebrows once a day in order to keep the hairs compactly together, training them to lie in the proper position. This gives a darker tint, and also avoids the untidy, straggling look that characterises some eyebrows. The treatment does not take more than three minutes, and the vaseline should be all carefully brushed off with another, and a perfectly dry, brush. The improvement will soon be distinctly apparent.

On no account omit to give attention to hair, teeth, face, and hands at night.

The night toilet.

Brush the hair several times, and then tie it in a loose plait. Warm water and a dry towel should be used on the face and hands, which should be rubbed with cold cream, to keep them white and soft ; and brush the teeth well.

CARE OF THE HANDS, ARMS, AND FEET.

Soft, white hands are always one of the principal points of a refined appearance, and for that reason women of all ages have most carefully tended their hands.

A mark of refinement.

The care of the hands cannot be said to be neglected nowadays, when both men and women make excellent incomes by acting as manicures. The operator scrapes the nails and makes them of a lively pink, pushes back the skin from the little white half-moons at the base, cuts the nails in a crescent which exactly follows the outline of the half-moons, and ends by washing the hands in a preparation that makes them both smooth and white, temporarily if not permanently. The hands look extremely well after the manicure's task has been finished, but there is a decidedly useless aspect about the long nails. The most beautiful hands are those that do little work. The long, tapering fingers are tipped with pink, and the nails are of the same rosy hue in the centre, with a milk-white crescent at the base, and a still whiter edge of nail at the tip. Erasmus Wilson says that the nails should never be scraped or cleaned with any instrument save

The manicure's art.

the nail-brush. The only other implement needed is the small ivory presser used to keep back the flesh from encroaching upon the nail.

The following mixture has been recommended for making the hands white : Upon a tablespoonful of scraped horse-radish, pour half a pint of hot milk. When this cools, bottle it, retaining the horse-radish in the milk. After having washed the hands, rub them over with this lotion, and then dab them dry with a soft towel. Glycerine used in the same way renders the skin smooth, and restores it where it has cracked and broken away under the influence of cold weather. If the hands are habitually dried with care, they will rarely need any such applications. A soft towel should always be kept on the towel-rail for the sole purpose of giving the finishing touch to the drying of the hands. An old huckaback is the best for this purpose.

To remove stains from the fingers, cut a raw potato, and rub a slice of it upon the marks. Chilblains are constitutional with some grown-up people, and when this is the case, they will come, notwithstanding every precaution. Directly they appear, they should be gently but thoroughly rubbed with spirits of turpentine, with which a few drops of the best. olive oil have been incorporated. This will prevent them

For white hands.

Finger-stains and chilblains.

from breaking, even if it does not drive them quite away. Chilblains are caused by defective circulation, and friction is the best remedy.

No woman should be without lemons on her toilet-table. They are about as necessary nowadays as soap, so those who believe in them say. Nothing in the world bleaches the skin, hands, and face like a little diluted lemon-juice applied at night, and, strange to say, unlike most bleaches, it softens the complexion. Then the finest of manicure acids is made by dropping a teaspoonful of lemon-juice in a cup of tepid water. This removes all stains from nails and skin, and loosens the cuticle naturally, and much better than any sharp instrument. A dash of lemon-juice (only a dash) in plain water is an excellent tooth wash, removing tartar, and a teaspoonful of the juice in a small cup of black coffee will drive off a bad headache.

The value of the lemon.

The hands soon show the effects of age, and one thing which much conduces to a premature shrinking of the muscles of the hand, and which is answerable for half the wrinkled palms and fingers we see at an age at which, normally, they should be fresh and firm, is that wretched habit of wearing gloves and sleeves that are too tight. Too-tight gloves especially must have their influence on the development of

Over-tight gloves.

83

the muscles wherever the circulation is defective.

The nails should be daily filed, but seldom cut. The eccentricity of wearing the nails long and pointed, like claws, should never be observed. The ideal nail is just long enough to protect the tip of the finger.

Filing the nails.

Thin arms should be as carefully concealed as though they were crimes. They have a half-starved, impoverished look that robs their owner of some of her dignity. They look very well in tight sleeves, it must be admitted, whereas fat arms look quite dreadful when squeezed into a similar kind of covering. Some arms are thin above the elbow, but quite prettily shaped below it. These look well in elbow sleeves, with a little lace or falling folds of net or lisse. If the arms are unduly long, as they occasionally are, the effect may be neutralised by wearing wide bands of black velvet fastened with pretty buttons or clasps, or buckles. This reduces the apparent length of the arms. " Thin arms," says M. Charles Blanc, the great French authority on dress, " denote bad health and an enfeebled race." My opinion is that they denote the folly of parents who allow their children to pass the first years of life in short sleeves. Red arms are ugly. I have noticed, of late, an enormous number of nutmeg-grater arms emerging and contrasting with

Thin arms.

sleeves in all the delicate shades of fashionable evening dress. They are red and rough. One can but wonder why. Are tight sleeves the cause? Or does tennis produce this unbecoming effect? The best remedy is to wash the arms with a fine lather of soap at least twice a day, and to dry **For rough skin.** them thoroughly and rub them vigorously. This treatment brings the pores into action, and induces a healthy condition of the skin, which disfavours specks and redness.

Rubbing with a soft chamois leather is excellent for the skin, giving it both smoothness and gloss. A **Chamois leather treatment.** girl who was much troubled with an eruptive disorder was advised to procure a very soft chamois leather and gently but persistently to rub the skin for a few moments daily. She did so, and never suffered from the same disfiguring cause again. The arms and shoulders are greatly improved by being rubbed in the same way; but the chamois must be very soft, or it will break the skin instead of polishing it.

Oil of almonds and almonds themselves are very good for the skin; the former is an excellent **Substitutes for soap.** substitute for cold-cream, and the latter crushed may be used instead of soap. A few drops of benzoin added to water and used as a lotion, keep the skin soft and prevent wrinkles prematurely appearing.

Lemon also may be used instead of soap. During the day it is better to rub the hands with a little than to use soap, and no manicure is ever required for hands thus treated.

Half a teaspoonful of the best glycerine mixed well with a little **To keep the hands white.** tepid water, and used daily, is supposed to keep the hands soft and white.

Take equal parts of white vinegar, spirits of turpentine, and the contents of an egg, and shake them **For chilblains.** well together in a bottle. Then rub this on gently. This is for unbroken ones.

For broken or unbroken chilblains an ointment, to be applied night and morning, can be made from benzoate of zinc, one scruple, mixed well with one ounce of fresh lard.

In washing the feet, observe that the water should not be very hot, which has a weakening tendency. **Washing the feet.** Cold water is invigorating, but the chill should be taken off for winter use. Once a week, the foot-bath should consist of warm water, and a good lather of soap should be made. The foot ought to be rubbed with a ball of sandstone, and afterwards dried with plenty of friction.

A box of sea-salt should have a corner to itself somewhere handy for use when chilblains threaten. Directly the skin

becomes inflamed, smarting when the
hands or feet invaded are cold, and
itching wildly when they are
hot, a solution should be prepared by throwing a hand-
ful of sea-salt into water and
allowing it to soak for an hour or two,
the water being just sufficient to cover
the salt. Then, with enough warm
water added to make the temperature
pleasant (the salt itself having been
strained away), a footbath should be
taken, the feet being very carefully
rubbed and dried after it. A fresh
infusion should be allowed to remain
all night and another footbath taken in
the morning. After that, the chilblains
will probably completely disappear.
I have never known this treatment
to fail with unbroken chilblains,
whether on hands or feet. A well-
known embrocation is the best means
of banishing them from the ears.

For preventing chilblains.

THE FIGURE.

" A native grace
Sat fair-proportioned on her polish'd limbs."
JAMES THOMSON.

" I will not dream of her tall or stately,
    She that I love may be fairy light ;
I will not say she must move sedately,
    Whatever she does will then be right.
Her air may be girlish, or matronly steady,
    Or that sweet calm that is just between !
But whenever she comes she will find me ready
    To do her homage, my queen, my queen."
OLD SONG.

THE charm of a good figure "needs no bush," and the amount of energy expended in mistaken efforts to attain it would, if heaped together and set unanimously in motion, suffice to move mountains. Thousands of women believe, even now, that a waist can never be too small, even for the largest and tallest figure. Proportion is wholly lost sight of in the endeavour to squeeze-in this portion of the frame, though success is occasionally rewarded with a terrible bulging of superfluous flesh above and below the waist line. Even at the best, a girlishly slender waist

Wasted energy.

Doubtful success.

88

goes badly with a mature figure. The average woman puts on flesh after the age of thirty. It is natural that she should do so; and the waist increases in size proportionately with the rest of the figure.

A natural development.

Without a good figure, it is almost impossible to be graceful of gesture.

"As the tongue speaketh to the ear, so the gesture speaketh to the eye."
                                        LORD BACON.

Gesture may be said to be the language of the body, as speech is that of the mind. The head, the arms, the hands, have an almost endless variety of gesture of their own. The French and Italian nations gesticulate to an extreme degree. The innate indolence of the Spaniard confines his gestures to those of a slow and lazy, but most expressive description. The Americans, full of energy and life, use more gesture than we do. The English, perhaps, gesticulate less than any other nation, but even with us there is more of it than is generally recognised. Joy and grief express themselves in gesture or attitude sometimes when the voice is powerless to do so. Where, otherwise, would be the power of pictures? Grace of gesture implies that of attitude. Graceful attitude, that is, implies grace of gesture as a

Gesture a language.

Gesture and attitude.

rule. When the body is trained to fall into harmonious lines, the gestures will follow those lines to a great extent.

That repose which marks the caste of Vere de Vere does not prevent the subtle innuendo conveyed by a scarcely perceptible shrug of the shoulders, an impatient movement of the head, languid though that movement may be. In moments of earnestness the most apathetic gives point to a denial by shaking the head, or to an affirmation by slightly bending it forward.

The best advice to give to those who would attain this grace is contained in two words : Avoid exaggeration. In the play of the limbs, as in that of the features, any approach to exaggeration is destructive to both features and effect. It is considered "bad style" to use much gesture, even in a quiet, subdued way, but when articulation is accompanied by unnecessary and too emphatic gesticulation the effect is of the most unpleasing kind.

Avoid exaggeration.

We all know how disappointing, if not actually annoying, it is to see a pretty face associated with an awkward figure or uncouth gait. Now, gracefulness is almost always cultivable, to some degree at least, in subjects, even, who might seem to be of the hopeless sort. Calisthenics have converted many an awkward girl into an un-

A charming acquirement.

recognisably graceful edition of her former self. Some girls need these artificial aids in an extraordinary degree, while others carry themselves well from childhood upwards.

Many a fast-growing girl has her figure and carriage ruined for life by want of care, and more particularly motherless girls, who have no kind elder to make them lie down for at least an hour every day. This is a very simple precaution against possible mischief, but its very simplicity causes it to be disregarded, as Naaman disregarded the Prophet's advice. But the recumbent posture averts many an evil. The shoulders should be perfectly flat upon the couch, and the head only slightly raised. If the girl likes to read while she is lying down, her book should be supported upon a reading-stand, and so placed that the light falls upon the pages from behind. Girls are such active, vigorous creatures that they often shirk the penalty — as it seems to them—of lying down in this way, but a loving mother knows what silent arts to employ in the matter, and how to turn the penance into a pleasure. But if the daily rest is omitted, the girl often becomes flat-chested, round-shouldered, awkward, and stooping, often crooked, and, realising her deficiencies, she is shy and uncomfortable, abashed and miserable, when she

Growing girls.

The penalty of neglect.

might have been bright, gay, and smiling in the presence of her mother's guests.

In any circumstances, improvement will result from gymnastic and calisthenic exercises, from rowing, drilling, and swimming. But it is absolutely necessary that the patient should be mindful constantly of her own bearing. She must hold her shoulders back, her head up (not her chin up), and her chest forward. At first this position should be studied before a mirror, when it will be found to be much more simple than it reads. In fact, it is only the ordinary attitude of a healthy child when standing erect. At first also its retention will involve some stiffness, but, if persevered in, and accompanied by calisthenic exercises, or even games like lawn-tennis, it will soon become natural, easy, and graceful. As there is often some cause for the loss of constitutional elasticity and vigour, from which round shoulders frequently proceed, this cause should be sought out and attended to. Simple exercises, admirably calculated to make the back strong and supple, are (1) swinging on the rings to be found in most gymnasia, (2) circling the horizontal bar, (3) bending forward and endeavouring to touch the toes, without flexing the knees, and alternating this action with an attempt to bend backwards with the arms outstretched above the head.

Gymnastic exercises.

With regard to roundness of the shoulders, various braces have been devised to hold the shoulders back. They are not entirely useless, but they must not be relied on to do more than encourage the patient to hold her spine erect, her head up, and her shoulders back actively.

Round shoulders.

Every girl who appreciates the value of a good figure and a graceful carriage of the arms should assiduously practice such exercises as moving the arms in a free circle from the shoulder, and should not be satisfied until she can get her shoulders into such a state of suppleness that she can touch together the backs of her hands behind her waist without rotating her arms inwards. (Rotation of the right arm or hand inwards is in the opposite direction to that taken by the hand in screwing in a gimlet or corkscrew.)

Some useful exercises.

For any one who can afford it, shampooing, or rather what is called massage, is highly beneficial to weak backs, stiff backs, and round shoulders. This is effected by an attendant and consists in vigorously kneading, rubbing, and pinching the soft structures on each side of the spine along its whole length, while the patient lies on the face. The process should be gone through once or twice a day, or oftener

Massage for weak backs.

in bad cases, and kept up for ten minutes at least each time.

Pigeon-breast is a disfigurement in which the front of the chest projects forward, and, at the same **Pigeon-breast.** time, the ribs, and the cartilages which unite them to the breast-bone, are flattened inwards in such a way as to produce a " keel " shape, bearing a superficial resemblance, so far as its prominence goes, to the breast of a bird. It is developed in childhood. It is believed to arise from obstruction to breathing during that period, *e.g.*, such as is caused by enlarged tonsils. It is sometimes, if not always, connected with rickets. Under favourable conditions there is a tendency to grow out of it to a certain extent. Gymnastics and exercise in the open air, and plenty of the latter, are chiefly to be recommended.

Narrow shoulders depend upon either a small chest or short clavicle (collar-bone), or upon both. **The shoulders.** They can be improved by exercises, more especially such as employ the arms and shoulders, namely, rowing, gymnastics, Indian clubs, &c.

Sloping shoulders can be made square by exercises which develop the chest.

High shoulders often depend on some habitual difficulty in breathing, which demands medical attendance. In almost any circumstances high shoulders will assume a better position if the patient will cultivate her "wind" by suitable exercises, and if she will, in addition, learn to carry her head properly, firmly, and freely.

Dr. Schofield, in a lecture on physical education in girls' schools, said that the evolution of the race imposes extra brain-service upon women and lays upon her a new physical strain. The body should be educated to meet this. He had been asked, he said, to condemn athletics, but he had to bless them. He did not, however, wish to see women with huge biceps. One of the best exercises for girls was to make six deep breathings and expirations each morning before dressing, but there should also be half an hour's athletic exercise daily. This would expand the chest, explore the recesses of the lungs, and increase the area of breathing space. Calisthenics for girls should cultivate graceful movement, and promote beauty as well as health and strength. In a London school, after athletic exercise, the floor was covered with buttons, until all the mothers discovered that all the dresses were deficient in chest-space. Athletics should not be indulged in by girls unless in gymnastic dress or dresses sufficiently loose. This should be remembered in regard to cycling by girls. Such an exercise should not

An expert on physical culture.

Appropriate clothing.

be taken except under conditions which leave full and free play to the lungs and the muscles, and this is applicable to all athletics.

Among open-air amusements there is no form of exercise pleasanter or more healthful for women *In praise of rowing.* than that of rowing. For women of ordinary physique, young or old, the exercise is not at all too heavy or violent ; it is easily limited, and the muscles of the arms and chest tend to good development. The skill shown in managing a boat gives an agreeable sense of power, and helps to create the feeling of independence and all-round ability to take care of herself which it is well for every woman to cultivate.

The conditions, also, in which rowing is done are all health-giving and pleasurable. The loose dress, without which no free or correct movements are possible, the open air and the changing scene which the boat makes possible are all provocative of quick-springing blood, and animated use, not only of the bodily powers but of *Vitality.* the mental. As a storer-up of vitality for the hard work which we all do at times, rowing is a wonderful agent. Vitality is the capital with which the business of life is done. And it is this good body, well developed in lungs, with firm muscles and steady nerves, that we women want to do our part of the world's work.

The advantage of having a good corset-maker who has studied anatomy is so patent that it need scarcely be insisted on. A cheap, ill-fitting corset of the so-called hygienic sort is often much more injurious than one that is well-cut and tight enough to fit the figure. The bones of a loose corset have a way of running into the chest that is not only very disagreeable and painful but also damaging. The cheap, ready-made corset is often too tight across the chest, and this is particularly injurious for growing girls. Cases of cancer have been traced to systematic constriction of this kind.

Corsets.

"Cheap and nasty."

Every now and then we read in some paper that tight-lacing is going out, and that natural figures are coming in. Where this statement originates it is impossible to guess. Do we believe it? Well, not exactly. We smile across the table at each other in the well-known, often-practised manner that expresses incredulity. Tight-lacing is not going out of fashion just yet, unfortunately. If everybody could afford to buy good corsets there might be some chance of its disappearing, but then everybody cannot, and when a girl gets one of those nasty, cheap ones at something three-farthings she puts it on, finds that her figure looks anyhow, and tries to make it right by

Tight-lacing and cheap corsets.

drawing it as tight at the waist as she possibly can.

Such a mistake ! With the ordinary lace the pressure is severe down the whole extent of the garment, for when the waist rebels against being unnaturally squeezed in the lace gradually widens at that point, and, of course, tightens above it. Consequently the chest is compressed and the breathing apparatus suffers, sometimes permanently.

Now, I am far from wishing to encourage tight-lacing, but if girls and women will practise it I should like to point out how it may be done with the least possible injury to the organs of the body. But I must repeat that in doing this it is under protest against tightening the stay-lace at all. However, girls (and women) will tight-lace, no matter what strength of protest is made, and it is better for them to do it in the least injurious way, if possible. Therefore I offer the following advice :—

Best use of a bad practice.

Instead of one long stay-lace, three shorter ones should be used. The top one should be carried down to a depth of about five eyelet holes, and there should be a bountiful provision of the lace left here, in order to give abundant breathing room to the lungs, permitting the chest to expand to the fullest, and allowing long, deep breaths to be drawn without that peculiar catch which denotes injurious tightness. There need be no exaggerated looseness, but only sufficient to afford perfect freedom from pressure. Instead of spoiling the look of the figure, this actually improves it.

The second lace should fill the eyelet holes below the first one down to the waist line, and should end there. It is sometimes, even, advisable to leave an eyelet hole on either side free from lacing, between the first and second stay-lace. But the object of the whole arrangement is to enable the second one to be drawn tight without squeezing-in the upper part of the figure in the least. And the third lace, in the same way, enables the wearer to avoid pressure on the hips, where it is highly injurious to some of the internal organs.

Of course, this is all unnecessary when funds are available to command a well-made corset from a trained physiologist, as are all really good corsetières, who fit the figure with exactest skill, and, without squeezing or tightening, give it a graceful outline. But with the cheap, ready-made article the above advice will, I believe, be found really useful.

I should like again to repeat that I wholly disapprove——but, no. I have said enough.

Well poised shoulders and erect carriage go far towards beauty. Many a comparatively plain girl makes more effect by these means than others better endowed as to face. The latter conveys an impression of good looks. The prettiness of the former *A good carriage.* has to be looked for and brought out. Very often a bad carriage comes of pure laziness. It is "too much trouble" to sit up straight, and it is "such a rest" to stand on one leg, with the other bent and curved into all sorts of impossible positions. Girls who indulge in these relaxations, all of which are bad for the health as well as antagonistic to beauty, should learn swimming, fencing, and dancing. All are valuable, fencing more than the other two. A little housework is to be recommended as efficacious, and the least expensive of all remedies. The vigorous use of a duster, the nice conduct of a broom, are excellent in their way, and a little digging in the garden is better still, and is also one of the best cosmetics in the world.

Even the prettiest face loses some of its attraction when it is accompanied *Stoutness.* by a heavy, bulky figure, fat out of all proportion to the head and face. This very ugly extreme is sometimes occasioned by ill-health, sometimes by a too sedentary life, and sometimes by self-indul- *The best remedy.* gence. It is best avoided by abstaining from eating more than is necessary and never drinking until a full hour after a meal.

There are numerous "cures" for over-development of flesh, and thousands of persons have reduced their bulk by following one or other of these. But, in making haste to be slender, many a women has sacrificed, most unintentionally, the prettiness of her face. Loss of good looks is a high price to pay for a slightness of figure which may, after all, be entirely disproportionate to one's age and circumstances. A word of warning may not be amiss.

Patent "cures."

A word of warning

There is a means of keeping flesh on the face while dieting it away from the body, but it involves the daily use of a quantity of cold cream or other fatty mixture, and this is sure to tell, in other ways, against good looks. A greasy, shiny skin is not at all desirable, yet this is what too much cold cream produces in many.

Cold cream and dieting.

The following advice for those who wish to decrease their weight has at least the merit of moderation: Lean meat (no fat), poultry, game and fish, toast, eggs, crust of bread, green vegetables and salads without oil. Beverages : Tea and coffee, with saccharine instead of sugar, and very little milk— no cream. No drink at lunch or dinner—but an hour after, lemonade, lime-juice, raspberry syrup, and other

Food for the Fat.

acid drinks; as little as possible of any. No alcohol; no wine; no beer, and very little milk. Plenty of exercise and hill-climbing, walking, running, riding, cricket, tennis, golf, &c.

For thin persons the following will be found efficacious. Fat beef, mutton, pork, &c. Thick soups with rice, tapioca, barley or bread in them. Plenty of good sweets—plenty of sugar in puddings —pastry, bread, butter, milk-puddings, sweet jellies, custards, creams, and all kinds of vegetables. Beverages: Tea, coffee, cocoa, chocolate, and milk. Thin persons may drink at meals; in fact, should make a practice of doing so. They should avoid pickles, acids of every kind (including sour wines), lemons, lemonade, salt meat, and salt fish. This generous diet gives much occupation to the digestive organs, and if they are not healthy it will do more harm than good.

Diet for the thin.

No thin woman can afford to lose her temper. Nothing so immediately induces scragginess. "Nothing," says a good authority, "will make you so angular or give your face such an undesirable look as the free indulgence of your own will."

Bad temper and good looks.

A girl who was thin to a really painful degree gained thirty pounds in sixty days on the following régime:— Twelve hours' sleep, no reading to be done during this half of the twenty-four hours. A well-ventilated room to sleep in, with lots of fresh air all night; **A régime for thin people.** light Jaeger blankets for warmth, and hot waterbags at the feet if they are cold, but a cold room. Loose, light clothing at all times, and plenty of space about the chest, shoulders, and waist; a diet of cereals, cocoa, fresh fruits, and starchy vegetables, potatoes, beans, peas, &c., milk, and cream—everything of a warming, fat-producing nature in the way of food; warm baths, though not too frequently; moderation in everything, work and play; plenty of outdoor exercise. Once you begin to rest and eat, the angles will give place to curves; and curves, if not too curv-y, spell good health and good temper.

One should sleep not merely six or eight hours a night, but until one wakes **Sleep.** refreshed. The time will vary with different women. Sleep restores the nervous power more than any other part of the system, and those who make the greatest drain on their nervous forces need the most sleep.

Sleeping without pillows under the head is said to be conducive not **Misuse of pillows.** only to sounder sleep, but to a more graceful carriage, and a stronger and straighter spine. The habit of placing large, heavy pillows under the head should never be contracted, and a medical authority says only a small, flat one should be used. Children should be taught to sleep on a flat, straight bed. A slight slope is not objectionable, and instead of using a pillow to make it, slip an extra slat or two under the frame of the spring mattress at the head, making the slope about three inches.

Breakfast should be nourishing, but not heavy, unless one is engaged in outdoor labour. The luncheon of indoor, and especially of brain, workers should also be very light. A heavy meal causes the blood to be withdrawn from other parts of the body to the stomach, there to do the work of digestion. If the brain also makes a demand upon the blood supply neither brain nor stomach is properly provided for, and the work of both is unsatisfactorily done.

Breakfast.

The morning bath should not be a lengthy affair, taken in a tubful of water. Such baths are temporarily enervating, tending to loss of flesh, and should be taken only when the bather has ample opportunity to recover from them. The morning bath should be taken standing in a few inches of water, and should be a shower or a sponge bath. It should be followed by a brisk rubbing with rough towels.

The morning bath.

ON BECOMING DRESS.

"Let never maiden think, however fair,
She is not fairer in new clothes than old."
TENNYSON'S "Enid."

"A native skill her simple robes express'd,
As with untutor'd elegance she dress'd;
The lads around admired so fair a sight,
And Phœbe felt, and felt she gave, delight."
GEORGE CRABBE.

THE influence of dress on good looks
has never been under-estimated by
women; and their realisa-
tion of its importance has
very largely affected the
trade and well-being of
nations. But it is probable that the
mistakes that are made in the art of
dress have gone as far to disfigure as
the successes to embellish. Do we
not, every day of our lives, see girls
and women who have garments and
headgear of such colour and form as
actually to rob the wearers of the share
of good looks they possess, instead of
heightening their effect?

Many a girl fancies that severity and
tailor-mades suit her best, when in
reality she needs softness
and frillery and all that
the dressmaker's art can do
for her. Masculine-looking
women are the better for being softened

down and feminised by flutter and furbelow, and it is on a womanly woman, a girlish girl, that tailor-mades look best. A boyish girl should avoid ultra-masculine styles, though by nature she inclines to them. They give her a hard, mannish air that is not attractive.

In the same way, those of short stature insist on wearing costumes that suit very well their taller sisters, but which have the effect of making themselves look a couple of inches shorter than they need. A shirt and skirt differing from each other in colour is one of the easiest ways of looking stumpy. Another is to wear a short coat with basques, and of a colour different from that of the dress. Checks also tend to apparently shorten the figure, while perpendicular stripes give it its full length, even a little over.

Styles for short people.

Horizontal lines have exactly the contrary effect. These should be avoided by stout persons, who can manage to look fairly slim by a deft arrangement of perpendicular stripes converging at the waist. They should never indulge in a breast-pocket, or any trimming that gives an extra look of width to the figure.

Stripes and checks.

In the same way, very thin, tall girls should adapt the cut and finish of their dresses and coats to suit their figures, and study the form of frills and the position of pockets with a special view to themselves. This does not require much time, and it **A hint to slender women.** is well worth some little trouble. A good dressmaker can always advise on such points.

As to colours, the effect they have on the appearance is so great that **On colours.** prudence in selection becomes one of the most important matters in costume. Bright colours make a stout woman look stouter, but give width and dignity to the thin. The fair of complexion may often wear yellow, amber, and orange, if the colour of the hair contains any hint of these tints. The usual colours for the blonde are pale blue, pale green, the lighter tones of cream colour, pale mauve, and a certain reddish tone of the same colour, deep wine-colours, and sapphire blue, if not too blue.

A green dress or hat throws its complement of red upon the face. If the **Colours and the complexion.** complexion be pale and deficient in ruddy freshness, or admits of having its rose-tint a little heightened, the green will improve it, though it should be delicate in order to preserve harmony of tone. But green changes the orange hue of the brunette into a disagreeable brick-red. If any green at all be used, in such case it should be dark. For the orange complexion of brunette the best colour is yellow. Its complementary, violet, neutralises the yellow of the orange and leaves the red, thus increasing the freshness of the complexion. If the skin be more yellow than orange, the complementary violet falling upon it changes it to a dull, pallid white. Blue imparts its complementary orange, which improves the yellow hair of the blondes, and enriches white complexions and light flesh tints. Blue is therefore the standard colour for a blonde, as yellow is for a brunette. But blue injures the brunette by deepening the orange, which was before too deep. Violet yellows the skin, and is inadmissible except where its tone is so deep as to whiten the complexion by contrast. Rose-red, by throwing green upon the complexion, impairs its freshness. Red is objectionable, unless it be sufficiently dark to whiten the face by contrast of tone. Orange makes light complexions blue, yellow ones green, and whitens the brunette. White, if without lustre, has a pleasant effect with light complexions ; but dark or bad complexions are made worse by its strong contrast. Pleated laces are not liable to this objection, for they reflect the light in such a way as to produce the same effect as grey.

The following colours suit a brown-haired, white-complexioned, tall girl :—Greenish blues, warm browns, peacock blue and green, dark red, pinkish grey,

Blue for blondes.

and certain soft shades of violet and mauve.

For a tall, thin girl, with light brown hair, dark eyebrows and lashes, and a not very good complexion, the following colours are best :—Warm browns and greys, and soft greyish shades of blue, not too light. Brighten up the greys or browns with pretty ribbons in soft tints.

A little jewellery, well chosen and really good, may be a distinct advantage to the appearance, but too much of it defeats its own end. Fingers crowded with rings to the knuckles are not admirable, and half a dozen bracelets plainly announce that their owner is fond of display.

Jewellery.

Earrings, once universally worn, are gradually becoming obsolete. There is no doubt that there is something barbaric in having holes drilled in the flesh for the sake of inserting ornaments.

Earrings.

The long earrings worn in the beginning of the Queen's reign were very disfiguring, pulling down the lobe of the ear and making the ornaments look more like instruments of torture than decorations. Even now, when they are quite small, it is difficult to forget that the piercing of a hole through the ear is necessary before they can be inserted, and the fashion which forbids earrings to be any longer worn is all on the side of common sense. At the same time, it

Fashionable barbarism.

must be admitted that a pair of beautiful, glittering earrings add a charming touch to a pretty face. Whether we think so because we are accustomed to them, or whether it is positively an improvement, it is difficult to say; but the impression remains that the two points of glittering light serve to frame in well-modelled cheeks, of fresh and dainty colouring, very appropriately. It was always a mistake to wear earrings with very large and ugly ears, and, in fact, the fashion lost some of its style by being adopted by women of every class.

A word for earrings

Gold or silver belts make the waist look large. Necklaces are very pretty additions to the toilette, but unless they are good, a piece of black velvet is better. There is no objection to really artistic imitations, some of which are triumphs of imitative skill, every pearl differing from the next in some detail of form or colour, just as do real pearls.

Belts and necklaces.

Jewellery ought to be kept locked up, for various obvious reasons. It needs careful cleaning now and then. Gold chains, bracelets, and earrings are best washed in a lather of soap and water, and well brushed with a hard brush kept for the purpose. If there are any stones in them, these must not be allowed to get damp, or they will become loosened from their settings.

The care of jewellery.

A dry brush should be kept for diamonds, sapphires, and so on, and occasionally applied to get **Cleaning precious stones.** the dust dislodged. When the stones are set clear, the brush should be used behind them as well as in front, with great advantage to the lustre of the gems. No one need fear to brush them well. The only thing to guard against is damp. A morning spent in cleaning and brushing up one's jewellery cannot be said to be misused, nor does it pass unpleasantly. This is lady's-maid's work, but it does not come amiss to lady's-maids' employers.

There is an old saying that the face suffers for every inch of neck uncovered by the dress. This **An old saying.** may possibly have some truth in it, but there is no doubt that a pretty, round, white throat looks charming with the dress cut away, and perhaps a row of pearls encircling it. *One row!* Anything beyond a single string detracts from the good effect.

As a rule, it is only the young throat that can with impunity be displayed in daylight by the dress being cut away. But there are exceptions to the rule, and one of the smartest women in London society, though a grandmother, wears her gowns in this fashion, and looks charming.

Tact in dress. Half the plain women in the world are plain because they do not know how to dress, nor what suits them.

Let no girl feel discouraged, however plain she may believe herself to be. There is such liberty in **For plain girls.** the matter of dress nowadays that she may make herself picturesque, if not entirely beautiful. But picturesqueness needs some study. Let no girl **Art and Anarchy.** fancy for a single moment that she may attain it by becoming—

" A rag and a bone and a hank of hair,"

like Rudyard Kipling's "Vampire." The warning might be considered unnecessary were it not for the numbers of girls one sees who have apparently taken that sketch for their model. A wild coiffure does not constitute picturesqueness, as many a mistaken girl seems to imagine. She may take counsel with an artist or a good dressmaker as to the style of dress that suits her, and, **A saving moderation.** having judiciously selected her style, carry it out with due regard to that moderation which is never more valuable than in matters relating to dress.

Alway wear easy shoes in the house, even if your vanity will not permit you to do so out of doors. The **On footwear.** toes will then enjoy some rest from pressure and will not grow as many corns and bunions as they would if it were continuous. High heels are a fruitful cause of corns, since they push the toes forward to the very edge of the boot or shoe. When the toes are pointed, matters are still worse. Could photographs be presented to our eyes of the feet of our different friends, many of them would be found to be records of pain suffered for the sake of vanity.

Young men who fall in love grow corns with reckless rapidity by squeezing their feet into boots **Tight boots and corns.** that are too small for them. Young maidens are equally reckless, whether they are in love or not. Young wives continue the weakness of their girlhood, in this matter, and their self-sacrifice is encouraged by an occasional remark from young husbands about pretty little feet. May they never grudge the money for new boots or the chiropodist's fee !

One of the great secrets of being well-dressed lies in taking care of one's clothes. Jackets must **Taking care of clothes.** be well brushed before being hung up, after having been worn. The skirts of dresses should be well shaken and then brushed. Bonnets and hats should be freed from dust, the feathers lightly blown, and the leaves of flowers picked daintily out with the fingers.

Gloves should never be folded in each other, but laid in a long box. Few of the glove-boxes sold are ever long enough to take a 12-button glove, and a nice present consists of a glove-box made to order, measuring from 20 to 22 inches in length. Glove sachets can easily be made at home, and impregnated with any favourite perfume. A long piece of satin, velvet, plush, or silk can be utilised for this purpose, lined with quilted satin and edged with silk cord. A spray of flowers painted on the outside would add to its appearance, and make it suitable for a present. Leather in pretty tints would be nice for this purpose, and it could be either embroidered or painted on.

How to keep gloves.

Neat boots are an important item in the wardrobe of the well-dressed. Many girls wear their boots too small, a practice which brings its own Nemesis in the shape of corns and bunions, which necessitate very large and roomy boots and shoes after a few years. Boots should be worn in turns, not day after day, as they so soon get out of shape. When cleaned they should be kept in a large box with the cover on. No room should be without a boot-bag. A large piece of holland suffices for the back, and several pockets, large enough to hold a pair of boots each, are sewn along the front. A deep valance depends from the top of the back and completely covers the openings to the pockets. This valance should be made five or six

Neat boots.

Boot bags.

inches longer than at first appears necessary, as when the pockets are filled they will require a longer valance to cover them. This boot-bag can be ornamented with pretty braid or thick washing lace. It is well when a good shop for boots has been found to always buy them there. It is also well to give a good price for them, though it need not be an extravagant one. The same advice applies to gloves ; much money is constantly thrown away on cheap gloves—there are women who cannot resist them. Though proof against alarming sacrifices in dresses, and desperate reductions in millinery, they cannot pass a shop where cheap gloves are exposed without investing. The odd thing is that, though the gloves never turn out satisfactory, these misguided bargain-hunters go on doing it. I know several who do.

For sponging silk in black or dark colours nothing is better than water in which the blue-bag has been **Sponging silk.** freely squeezed, until it is of a dark blue tint throughout. The sponge (perfectly clean) must be wrung tightly out of this, so that too much moisture may not be applied to the silk. For taking grease spots out of woollen material rock ammonia dissolved in boiling water is effectual. Sponge the cashmere, serge, or homespun with this as hot as the hand can bear it. When dress materials of any kind have been sponged they should not be dried by the fire, but in the open air, when possible, or in a warm room a long way from the fire. If they dry too quickly they are inclined to shrink, which spoils their appearance. Soda, used in the same way, is a fair substitute for ammonia. Benzoin is occasionally found useful for extracting stains, but it sometimes deprives the fabric of its colour.

The time-honoured proverb about having a place for everything and keeping everything in its *The virtue of tidiness.* place is never better justified of its wisdom than with reference to matters of dress. It is the small things that suffer most from carelessness and forgetfulness in this department. Veils, fichus, neckbands of silk, ribbon, or muslin, collars, whether of lace or embroidery, if not kept tidily, are apt to be turned over in the wild rush of finding something at the last moment when hurriedly preparing for a walk or drive with the dreadful consciousness that the others are all ready and waiting for us. At such moments one "makes hay" on the shelves of one's wardrobes, and I have known a chest of drawers, after some such hasty search, to suggest a recent earthquake, with the contents all hanging out of the various drawers, and looking at least twice as much as the latter could possibly contain. Veils get sadly depressed in such circumstances, and very often fail completely to recover from the effects of violent treatment. Each should be pinned, after wear, in or on a piece of folded tissue paper, in the same way as the fringe nets are, when sold. Lace and embroidery made into fichus and collars should be delicately shaken out, and then lightly folded and laid away where no one is likely to forget their whereabouts and bestow a heavy bodice on top of them. Accordeon-pleated blouses or skirts should always be laid away at full length. It spoils the hang of the pleating to fold them back. There should be a separate box or drawer or shelf for neck ribbons or folded draperies of silk or chiffon for the neck. They should be wrapped in tissue paper if white. Steel or jewelled buttons should never be put away—even when sewn on gowns or belts—without being wrapped closely, each in a wisp of tissue paper. This will protect them from rust or loss of brilliancy.

To wash coloured dresses, have ready plenty of clean, soft water ; it spoils coloured clothes to wash them in the dirty suds the white clothes have been washed in. The water should be warm, but not sufficiently hot to injure the colours. Rub enough soap in the water to make a strong lather before the coloured articles are put in.

Washing coloured dresses.

Wash them thoroughly; then a second time in clean, warm suds, and rinse them well. Have ready a pan filled with weak starch, and tinged with a little blue. Printed lawns, muslins, and cambrics will be much improved by mixing a little gum-arabic water with the starch, about a tablespoonful. Run the stuff through the starch, then squeeze it out, open it well, clap it, and hang it out immediately to dry in the shade. If coloured clothes continue wet too long no precaution can prevent the colours from running into streaks. This will certainly happen if they are allowed to remain too long in the water. If the colours are once injured nothing can restore them; but by management this may always be prevented, except in coarse, low-priced calicoes (though many of these wash perfectly well). As soon as the dress is quite dry take it in. It is always the best way to fold and iron it immediately. Another way of fixing the colours in a dress is to grate raw potatoes into the water in which the dress is washed. If dresses are to be put by for a winter season they should always be washed and dried, but not starched or ironed, and should be rolled up closely in a towel.

Summer washing dresses are often very well done up by the laundresses, but sometimes failure is disastrous. It is usually safer to send them to the cleaner, and more especially when they are trimmed with lace or fine embroidery, or if the colour happens to be very delicate. Blouses **Summer dresses.** are sometimes carelessly sent to the wash when a little consideration would have shown the sender that none of the ordinary processes of washing could be applied with any chance of success to the trimming. Lace laid on in rows, for instance, cannot be ironed on the wrong side, the only way that makes it look even passable after having been washed. A little trouble in unpicking it beforehand would in such cases be well worth while.

For a small noise the squeaking of shoes is most annoying and a trial to one's nerves. Procure a **Squeaking shoes.** small gimlet, and from the inside bore a hole half way through the sole of the shoe. This makes an outlet of escape for the air confined between the layers of leather of which the sole is composed, and is the cause of the disagreeable noise.

The seaside ruins black shoes. None but white or brown ones should be worn there, whether the **Seaside hints.** locality be chalky or sandy. Each is destructive in its way, and also to the hems of gowns. Moral : Wear your skirts well off the ground. Nor is there any necessity to lengthen them again on returning to town ! All the sensible women wear their walking

119   9

gowns a good inch off the ground all round.

Patchouli is a preservative against moths. The Indian shawls were perfumed with it, and thus it became known in Europe. Kept with linen or wool, no moths will go near it.

Patchouli for moths.

To make laces or handkerchiefs after washing look perfectly new, wash them as clean as you can, putting a very little blue into the water if necessary, rinse them repeatedly, and then plaster them up on the mirror or against the window pane to dry. In spreading them out on the glass, pull all the embroidered edges evenly, and see that the square of cambric sets straight and even. When they get dry, and are peeled off the glass, they will have the smooth transparency and peculiar gloss of lawn which has never been washed, and every leaf and flower of the embroidery will stand out clear and distinct, the worked initials looking like raised letters on the pure white background.

Washing laces and handkerchiefs.

The best dressing for black shoes and boots, as we have often been told, is orange juice. Take a slice or quarter of an orange and rub it on the shoe or boot; then, when the shoe is dry, brush it with a soft brush until it shines like a looking-glass. Another fruit dressing for tan shoes is the inside of a banana

Fruit as boot cleaners.

skin. Rub the skin all over the shoe thoroughly, wipe it off carefully with a soft cloth, and polish the shoe with a flannel cloth briskly. Patent leather shoes should not be polished with blacking. These are the most difficult kind of shoes to keep in good order, and require constant care. They may be cleaned with a damp sponge and immediately dried with a soft cloth, with occasionally a little vaseline or sweet oil.

From light materials grease stains can be removed by pressing a hot iron over blotting-paper laid on the spot. If this is not quite effectual a little hot water and ammonia may finish the work; but with light materials great care is required.

Grease stains.

Never choose a cheap veil, or one with many spots. Both are extremely bad for the eyes.

Veils.

Prepared borax is invaluable for softening the hardest water, whether from pump, tap, river, or sea. One tablespoonful is sufficient for a gallon of water, and it will save much more than its cost in soap, labour, and time, while it prevents the destruction of fabrics, making them "white as snow and sweet as new-mown hay"—important results alike in table and toilet linen.

Borax for washing.

For washing lace, muslin, ribbon, and such fine articles, use a tablespoonful of borax to every pint of water, and soak the articles for twenty-four hours; then wash them, **For lace and fine articles.** and the dirt will be found to drop out almost without rubbing.

Straw and chip hats are much improved by being washed in **Straw hats.** a solution of borax.

To freshen black lace lay it on a clean board, moisten it all over with a piece of old black silk **Black lace.** dipped in a teaspoonful of borax in a pint of water, and while the lace is damp cover it with a piece of black silk or cloth, and iron it.

For starching, put between one and two teaspoonfuls of borax to every pint of boiling starch; stir **Starching.** it till it is dissolved; this imparts a gloss to the articles.

A cold solution, made by adding a tablespoonful of borax to the water in the toilet bottle makes an **Mouth wash.** excellent mouth wash, and keeps the bottle sweet and clean for years.

To clean black kid gloves mix a few drops of black ink with a **Black kid gloves.** teaspoonful of salad oil. Apply it with a feather, and dry the gloves in the sun.

It is not wear, but lack of care that makes a bedraggled mass of one's best gown in a couple of months, **The care of clothes.** and often it suffers most when not being worn. The way shopkeepers care for ready-made garments is an excellent object lesson. Coat hangers are cheap, but half a barrel hoop, linen wound, with a loop in the middle, is even cheaper, and answers the purpose as well. These are for heavy skirts, bodices, and jackets. Thin garments should be folded with light paper stuffed in sleeves and bows.

Women are not so much addicted to the use of the clothes-brush as men are. It is regrettable that **The use of the clothes-brush.** it should be so, for nothing keeps clothes in better order than regular brushing. Coats, jackets, and woollen gowns need an application after every time of wearing. Silks should never be brushed, but if they are very dusty a good **Brushing silks.** plan is to fasten a piece of crape round a clothes-brush and brush the silk with that. This also takes the dust from velvet very quickly. A soft bonnet-brush should always be kept in a little case on purpose for bonnets and hats. Collars should be kept in a round collar box with a little pocket at the side for studs, clasps, &c.

To have well-fitting clothes is one of the points by which a gentlewoman is distinguished from her **Well-fitting clothes.** lowlier sisters. It is not so easy a matter as might be imagined, needing a little thought and care, and the expenditure of a great deal of money. Skill is costly, and only skill can compass the exactitude of fit that has now become one of the first exigencies of fashion. The trifling modifications of this year's modes, as compared with those of last, have to be copied. Those who are neither extravagant nor very rich find that there are nearly always certain alterations needed to adapt them to the present, and here is one of the occasions when a nimble needle and a knowledge of dressmaking are extremely useful. To make a dress fit into the newer, fresher styles, and also fit the figure, whether it has grown slighter or stouter, is not always an easy thing. Maids, with the aid of a **Dress stands.** mannequin, sometimes accomplish it, but they dislike the task, and usually take an unconscionably long time over it. The mannequin, or dress-stand, being a wire frame, with the bodice made to the measurements of one's own, is an excellent institution. It enables one to dispense with much of that disagreeable business, trying on, and to arrange draperies in a manner which would be impossible on one's own figure.

To those who wish to keep their hats up to the standard without a **Hints on millinery.** great outlay of money or constant recourse to Mme. Milliner, the practical hints given in classes by a first-class teacher of millinery may prove worthy of consideration. The best velveteen, says an authority who knows, is better than silk velvet, so far as durability and keeping in order are concerned, for making or trimming hats. Rain will not spoil a good quality of velveteen, and a little steaming will make it as good as new, while a few drops of water on silk velvet make little indentations hard to remove.

For black hats, chip or straw, beginning to grow rusty, liquid shoe polish may be used to good advantage. Hats should be brushed every day before laying them aside to keep the dust from grinding in. Artificial flowers drooping and crushed may be brightened and freshened **Flowers and feathers.** by shaking them for ten minutes through the steam from a boiling tea kettle. Ostrich feathers respond to the same treatment. A good quality of ribbon makes the most durable and consequently cheapest of all hat trimmings, standing the moisture of the sea or flying dust of streets or country driving better than flowers, feathers, or lace.

Steel ornaments may be made as good as new by scrubbing them in hot soapsuds, using a nailbrush to reach the interstices, then polishing them with a chamois or drying in sawdust. To renovate old **Renovating thread lace.** black thread or French laces dip them into a solution of weak green tea, then spread them out upon several thicknesses of newspaper laid upon the ironing board or other flat surface. With a pin pick out each little point or scallop, cover the lace with sheets of newspapers, and put a weight on the paper, allowing it to remain twenty-four hours.

Fine white laces, delicate ribbons and silks may be freshened and cleaned with powdered magnesia, or, **Magnesia for fine fabrics.** if not too badly soiled, with hot flour—taking care that it is not browned in the heating. Sprinkle the magnesia or flour upon a smooth sheet of wrapping paper, lay the silk or lace upon the paper, and sprinkle more magnesia over it. Cover it with another sheet of paper, place a book or some light weight on the paper, letting it rest there for several days. Take the fabric up, shake it well and brush it with a soft brush. For laces that require stiffening rinse them in a pint of water, in which a piece of gum-arabic the size of a pea is dissolved, roll them round a bottle, and pull or pat them with a soft towel until dry.

UNWIN BROTHERS, PRINTERS, WOKING AND LONDON.

MANNERS FOR MILLIONAIRES

Manners for Millionaires answers the cry for instruction and guidance from the aspiring rich. Following the course from penury to plenty, this book is intended to help readers ascend the staircase of Prosperity.

'As the French say, if you wish to be riche you must start de nouveau.'

Hardback £7.99

ISBN 978 0 7123 5724 1

THE FINISHING TOUCH
Cosmetics through the Ages

Julian Walker

This fascinating new book explores some of the materials and methods that women – and men – have used in the past to enhance or hold on to their looks. Julian Walker opens up a curious, sometimes uncomfortable history of the human need to look beautiful. He reveals dozens of the (occasionally desperate) ways in which people have tried to make themselves more attractive. The book tells a story of ingenuity and imagination, but also of self-delusion, trickery and exploitation.

Hardback £10
ISBN 978 0 7123 5752 4